CODEPENDENCY

RECOVERY

WORKBOOK

A Comprehensive Beginner's Guide to Recognize and Break
Free from Codependent Relationships, Stop People Pleasing
and Recover from Unhealthy Relationships

JESSICA TYLER

Table of Contents

Introduction

So, you just found out you're codependent and ready to break free from that. What do you do? Being codependent is a very tough situation that affects everything you do in life in ways that are far from awesome. You may have noticed that you've struggled not to control others because you feel out of control, and you want nothing more than to stop being bugged down by the pain and resentment you feel. Is there any way to set yourself free, you wonder? By choosing this workbook, you've made the best first step possible.

Let's face it: Codependency sucks. Also, not everyone is a narcissist. Codependents, people who have been mistreated in the past, and people who have had to put their own needs last for a long time may be victims of abuse and social conditioning without giving into the destructive cravings for power and control that are inherent in addiction.

Codependency can destroy relationships because it is built on fear and withholding love from others, which doesn't motivate them to give you what you need from them. It can cause physical damage as well as mental anguish. Codependent individuals often feel out of control when their boundaries are crossed, and they struggle with self-esteem issues due ultimately to the neglect brought upon them by those around them.

1

Codependence is a learned survival strategy, but it is also an addiction. In this workbook, you will learn how to take your life back and discover who you are outside codependency's confines. Unlike other books, this one won't confuse codependency with love. We will look at it for what it is and change your course for the better. Everything is written in simple English for you to clearly understand the concept of codependency and what you can do about it.

You will understand why you do the things you do and how to change them. You'll learn how to calm your anxiety, stop the denial, and take a look at yourself in a new light, one that isn't so full of self-doubt and low self-esteem. You'll learn that being codependent is not an acceptable way of life, regardless of what your family taught you or what has happened to you. You'll also take back your power and learn how to use it to better yourself and help others.

This workbook will allow you to look at codependency from the perspective of the codependent and what makes them tick. It will also show you that, no matter what your past has been like, you can change and move on to harbor new relationships that are healthy and rewarding for everyone involved. Instead of trying to control everyone, you can finally start living a happy life without depending on someone else for approval or love.

Chapter 1

What Is Codependency
and How Do You Fix It?

In this chapter, you're going to discover the true meaning of codependency since there are far too many takes on the matter that are far from accurate. You'll learn a bit about addiction because there's usually a connection between that and codependency for both parties. You'll also discover what Cognitive Behavioral Therapy is and why you need to take your life back. As you read, you need to remember that your ultimate goal isn't just breaking free from codependence but achieving healthy, functional interdependence. What's that? You'll know you've achieved it when you come to lean on yourself as an adult when it comes to the basic wants and needs you have while at the same time being open to having others support you and satisfy the needs that only they can. This way, you allow the other person in the relationship to take care of themselves while at the same time being supportive. This is the opposite of one person always carrying the other until they lose it.

What Is Codependency?

For the most part, there's a lot of confusion surrounding the term codependency, and this is because the *Diagnostic and Statistical Manual of Mental Disorders* or DSM-5 doesn't list it as a disorder. This is the reference used by most mental healthcare providers in the United States of America to help diagnose mental disorders and figure out the symptoms. The fact that codependency isn't listed in the manual makes it difficult to explain what it is and how it manifests.

If there's one thing you can always spot in the manifestation of codependence, the codependent person has an external point or locus of focus on the world. This means they don't have intrinsic self-worth and therefore need to look to things outside themselves to feel validated. They need others to let them know what they're worth.

The codependent doesn't believe they deserve anything good, so they turn to everything outside of them to prove that they are indeed worthy of their existence. On the other hand, interdependency involves an internal focus on yourself where you know you're worthy and capable. You have a healthy sense of self-esteem, and this is why you tend to act in ways that show you're mature, respectable, and aware of who you are.

Regarding codependency, the problem isn't about being concerned for others' well-being. The concern is how much you might neglect yourself terribly while being there for someone else and tending to their every need. It's natural human behavior to express concern for others' well-being and to do and say things that indicate we care. Being human means interdependency is hardwired in one and all. However, codependency takes caring and connecting with others several steps too far, completely consuming your everyday life.

Thankfully, more and more people are becoming aware of codependency, and several experts understand the issue. Thanks to research, it is clear that codependency has several symptoms you can use to identify it, whether in a family or a romantic relationship. The codependent symptoms remain consistent across the board. It's also not unusual to have intense attraction between codependents, as the way their symptoms are set up, it would be hard to resist the pull. It's also been found that codependents are likely to hate someone they think is toxic but have no awareness of how their own behaviors contribute to the relationship's toxicity. These people aren't aware of their own thoughts, emotions, attitudes, and insecurities, so they can't see how they act as enablers for the toxic person they're in a relationship with.

Two Faces

There are two ways codependency presents itself, one being more familiar than the other. The first form involves constant caretaking and an intense need to please people, while the second has the codependent person feeling entitled and selfish. This selfish codependent acts in a way that could lead one to assume that they're really a narcissist, as they always have the impression that the life they have should be much easier and better than it is. Rather than feel worthless or insecure, this codependent goes through life with the assumption that they're the cream of the crop, far above and beyond everyone else. When codependency presents in this selfish and entitled form, the odds that the codependent will seek help are very low because it would cost them their ego. As for the people who live and interact with them, they suffer as a result and usually wind up presenting codependence in the form of trying to please the entitled codependent.

Where Does It Begin?

Codependency results from childhood trauma, where even as an adult, you're immature. Trauma is from the Greek word for "wound." Most codependents do their best not to blame their problems on their parents, but the fact remains that they definitely had the wound when they were kids. However, there are certain cases where a child had a good upbringing but grew up and became codependent due to adulthood trauma such as infidelity or physical and sexual assault.

It's important to state that codependency is not the same as Post Traumatic Stress Disorder or PTSD. The latter has unique symptoms that appear in a cluster and some physiological effects that aren't part of codependency.

There are childhood traumas that are, sadly, all too common contributors to becoming codependent. Among these traumas are:

- Growing up in a home where one or both parents are addicts or alcoholics/

- Having a parent struggling with mental illness that they may or may not be aware of.

- Needing to put on a mask or play some role as a child instead of being who you really are.

Regarding the previous trauma, it's sad that some families will require children to play specific roles, especially when said family is troubled. Here are some of the roles you may have had to play:

- **The one who placates**: In this case, the child learns that they're only there to help others feel better rather than express how they feel or think.

- **The one who saves**: The golden child always comes to the rescue to save the family's face. They can do no wrong, and when they do, those wrongs are often blamed on someone else in the family.

- **The one who takes the blame**: The scapegoat is, in the family's mind, the one responsible for every bad thing to befall them. If something terrible happens, the scapegoat is the first to blame.

- **The one who's invisible**: This is a child who is not there. They're present, but no one acknowledges them, and they're often left to their own devices and neglected.

- **The one who makes them laugh**: This is the jester, the one who can make the family feel relief through laughter, comedy, and joy.

Regarding roles, it's important to state that you may have worn different masks simultaneously. For instance, you may have been the golden child to your father and the scapegoat to your mother, and this would have caused you to feel confused about who you really are. In this case, it's little wonder you don't know your worth. You may not see yourself as having played any of these characters, but codependency is rooted in past wounds.

Codependency in Relationships

To be clear, you don't need to be in a situation with alcoholism or drug addiction before experiencing codependency. It can appear in all relationships, whether between friends, siblings, parents, and their children, etc. Regarding romantic relationships, codependency tends to appear stronger than in any other situation, to the point where it could be considered an addiction to love — a phenomenon that is also not in the DSM-5. Love addiction is a concept that Stanton Peele branded in *Love and Addiction,* which he published in 1975. In it, he noted that love is the fuel for addiction because of its ability to take over your consciousness completely. For something to become an addiction, it has to act as a source of reassurance and consume all of one's time, money, energy, and other resources. Therefore, sex and love are the perfect fodder to feed the flames of addiction.

Dr. Helen Fisher led a team of researchers to look into what happens on a chemical level in the brain when one is in love. The team found that when you fall in love, your brain contains norepinephrine and dopamine. The latter drives you to seek out the things you find rewarding and pleasurable, while the former causes your heart rate to spike and gives you the rush to be loved and in life. It turns out these are the same neurochemicals the brain produces excessively when on cocaine, but love's high lasts longer than a bump. With this in mind, it's clear how a relationship could easily become an addiction.

According to Pia Mellody, a well-known expert on codependency, love addiction tends to happen between two distinct people: The love addict and the love-avoidant. The love addict tends to fall not for the person they're with but for an idealized version of them in their mind.

This makes it tough to see the person they're with for who they really are, making it harder to break free from the addiction. It's akin to placing the other person on a pedestal and calling them God. The love addict gets a rush from their fantasies about the love-avoidant, and they're often only thinking about when next they get to be with them or how to be with them more often. If you asked the love addict, they would tell you they desire to merge with the other person, seeing them as a savior who could rescue them from themselves.

As for the love-avoidant person, they tend to be more about themselves in their codependency and put on a good show, not being their true self. They put up walls around them that make the love addict fall even deeper for the perceived air of mystery around them. For the love-avoidant, love is about being needed. So, they feel drawn to the love addict, and yet they also resent them. So, they actively seek things and people that can distract them from their relationship. They could engage in infidelity or turn all their focus on work so that the love addict doesn't get too close to them.

The Connection between Addiction and Codependency

Addiction and codependency have been involved in an intricate tango for the longest time. The first time the word "codependent" came to be, was thanks to a German psychiatrist, Dr. Karen Horney, from the 1800s. It picked up in popularity and a description for those involved with alcoholics in a relationship. Before codependency was officially identified, the professionals of those times noted that when it came to addiction, the family members acted in a way that tended to exacerbate the addiction or keep their loved one from recovering.

However, this doesn't mean that addiction and codependency are the same processes.

Codependency can present as a standalone situation. However, there are several reasons it can and does bleed into the struggle of addiction. For one thing, being in a relationship with someone struggling with alcohol and other drugs naturally draws the codependent person, making them want to invest their energy, time, money, attention, and every resource at their disposal in this person they want to "save." It helps them to know that they have a way to show that they're worth something: By how well the codependent can take care of the addict and whether they can help them do better. The other thing to consider is that life as a codependent is tough, so it's natural to have some sort of addiction to a substance or behavior to keep the pain in check. For instance, the codependent may not be able to see how they are also an addict. This is because they're focused on the person outside of them. So, they assume that whatever issues they may have been caused by others who may have made them feel like they're not needed or made them feel hurt, disappointed, or angry. In this codependent's mind, everyone else is the problem. They can't see how they're choosing how to cope with life.

Those in addicted codependency tend to either act as the addict or the enabler. As the enabler, they're all about keeping the addicted person safe from the expected consequences of their addiction. They do this from a place of love in their minds. They're the ones you can expect to cover up for their drunk lover who just got in another accident by saying it was them behind the wheel. They're likely to explain to their kids that their dad only yelled and got upset with them because it was their fault, not his. The enabler shields the addict so that the latter never has to deal with consequences and therefore has no reason to change, thus fueling more addiction.

The addict in this scenario may know how to control others using their addiction. For instance, they could decide that discussing what's going on with work and money is a big no because it would trigger them into giving in to their addiction. This is a form of manipulation, and they could use that to make the enabler handle the financial duties in the family. The addict will weaponize their addiction if it gets them what they want.

Addiction

According to Pia Mellody in Facing Love Addiction, a person with an indication may be codependent, and a codependent person likely has a few obsessive-compulsive and addictive mental processes. Addiction is as confusing as codependency is, especially in terms of psychology. There's also the extra difficulty of the stigma that accompanies addiction due to looking at it through the lenses of morality and race. It doesn't help that far too many agree with Dr. Benjamin Rush's sentiment about how alcoholism is a matter of will. Many assume that all addiction is a result of having a weak will, of being too lazy to want to change things. This is part of the problem with codependency. Some codependents erroneously assume that the addict they're with is deliberately choosing their substance of choice over them and that if they (the codependent) could improve in some way, they would finally be enough for the addict to choose them instead. However, codependency involves constant denial and making big issues seem less problematic than they are. When the codependent thinks addiction is a matter of will, it only adds to their denial of their situation. This problem is also why you may see a codependent judge someone for indulging in substances or bad behavior, only to do the same thing themselves.

Fortunately, addiction is now viewed through science instead of morals. Therefore, it's clear from the research that there are physiological changes in the brain due to substance abuse, so addiction is not a matter of will but a brain disease. Addiction is a result of dysfunction in the circuits of the brain that have to do with reward, motivation, and memory, among other things. This dysfunction shows up socially, spiritually, psychologically, and biologically as the addict seeks relief and reward by consistently using substances or engaging in harmful behavior. The addict, therefore, cannot stay away from their addictions constantly, control their impulses, suffer from ruined relationships, and not get a hold of their emotions. Addiction is so problematic that remission can't be celebrated without worrying that there's a relapse around the corner, and when the addict doesn't get treatment or recover, it could lead to total mental disability or death. In the DSM-5, the processes linked to addiction are known as "Substance-Related Disorders."

Codependency and addiction have trauma in common. Also, if substance use is terribly frequent, there's a higher chance that PTSD will occur since the addiction can fuel sexual, emotional, and physical abuse. There's also an interesting connection between food addiction and trauma, as the more traumatic one's experience is, the more likely they are to consume soda and fast food. Women with PTSD are two times more likely to struggle with food issues than those without PTSD.

CBT: Good for Codependency

CBT focuses on the usual distortions in thought and other cognitive processes responsible for holding up the issue you're struggling with: Codependency. Distortions are filters that are overlaid on your way of thinking that cause you to act as codependent. The typical codependent may not be aware of it, but many errors in their thought processes add more fuel to the fires of resentment, pain, and the plight of codependency itself. For instance, the codependent may feel like it's horrible for them to have any interest in their own affairs and well-being. So whenever they feel the need to care for themselves or be kind to themselves by taking it easy, they wind up feeling guilty for having that thought, let alone acting on it. The usual way people handle the guilt is by flat-out denial, as they tell themselves that there's no need to take care of themselves and refocus their energy on someone else's needs.

In Cognitive Behavioral Therapy or CBT, it's known that events can trigger thoughts and that the events in a codependent's life are different from someone who's interdependent. For instance, a codependent person may get the sense that they're always the ones picking up after everyone else, making them feel angry and resentful. Then they display their displeasure in passive-aggressive ways, validating their behavior as being the other person's fault. For an interdependent person, they'd just assume, despite their irritation with the mess they see, that there's a good reason no one else could clean up. They don't take it personally, meaning they don't display any passive-aggressive vengeance. They could decide it's important to speak to everyone at home about being tidier, but that's about it.

The rollercoaster ride of codependency is driven by thoughts that aren't accurate or helpful. The constant focus on what's outside of you can make it seem like you never have a choice other than to be at others' mercy, constantly being victimized, but this isn't true. The truth is, unless it turns out you're in an actual terrible situation like an abusive marriage or other relationship, no one else affects your life other than you. You're in charge, even if you think you aren't. You only feel like you're not because you have a certain way of viewing life that causes you to act in ways that only make it seem even more like you are a victim. So, your journey, breaking through codependency, is to remind yourself that you've always got a choice and are responsible for making it alone.

CBT is a great way to help you find the truth about your beliefs and thoughts that drive codependency and make you feel stuck. It's like your brain has been stuck in a groove, and you can jar it out of that unproductive, well-worn grove by paying more attention to the distortions in your thinking and the untruth in your beliefs, as well as looking at new ways of seeing things. This is the power of CBT, showing you that you always have a choice regarding your reactions and that even when you can't because things have escalated terribly, you can always take a break. With CBT, you can break free of the impression that you're being controlled or manipulated by others. This means you're no longer a victim. You're free.

The road to freedom is long, and it's not something accomplished overnight. So, you have to be kind to yourself as you recover from codependency. Remember, through the lens of CBT, every action you take has a logical purpose, and your actions are likely because of your childhood or even adulthood wound. So, you need to be gentle with yourself when you notice your old patterns coming up for air. Also, note that you must be willing to change to see good results. You will be the best cheerleader you have as you journal and work with the exercises in this workbook. Note that this workbook is only a resource, but it's not a stand-in for professional therapy if you need it. You'll know you need therapy if you're experiencing anxiety, depression, and suicidal ideation. If you're also struggling with addiction in your relationship, you might find it best to work with a therapist.

Chapter 2

Recognizing the Patterns

Codependency involves patterns of thought and behavior that are counterproductive to the point of being destructive. When you keep following these patterns, they only create more pain and resentment, and on top of that, it makes you feel unworthy. You'll learn how to master these patterns and break free from them. First, you've got to develop awareness to see how you continue to keep yourself codependent. This way, you'll be able to change what needs to change so you can be better.

Traits of Codependency

As a codependent person, there are certain belief systems you have that do not serve you, and these are often made even clearer by the relationships you are in, which can make them even worse. Codependency tends to show up in unique ways, but certain traits are common to one and all. For instance, according to CBT, you can expect distortion in thinking or cognitive distortion. Among these are:

- Black and white thinking.

- Personalization.

- "Should" or "must" declarations.

Regarding black-and-white thinking, the codependent person assumes that there are only two options to pick from. It never occurs to them that actually there is a spectrum of choices. As for personalization, the codependent person has a habit of taking other people's bad behavior personally. When someone treats them poorly, they take that as a sign that they are not worthy. Finally, there are declarations of how people should or must act in certain ways. In the codependent person's mind, if you do not fall in line, you should face the consequences, which are often exaggerated.

Here's how all three traits tend to play out in relationships plagued by codependency and sometimes addiction. The codependent person may conclude that their loved one has to stop abusing a certain substance and that the only option available for this person is to completely abstain and get treatment. Inevitably, the addicts decide they will not go with that program. Then the codependent person might assume that means that they aren't worth it. They genuinely believe that they are not worth the efforts of change. After all, if they were worthy of love, wouldn't their dear one agree to go for treatment and completely stop using drugs? This means there's no way the relationship can be salvaged — at least, in the codependent's mind.

Codependents struggle with intimacy. It's impossible to have healthy relationships when you continue to make other people's choices a statement of your worth or try to control them based on what you think is good for them.

No Sense of Self

Have you ever felt like you don't know who you are? Then the odds are you are dealing with codependency, even if you're unsure what your symptoms are. Not knowing who you are or feeling lost is par for the course. This is due to the role-playing you had to endure in your family, which kept you confined to thinking, being, and expressing yourself in certain ways. When the role is no longer required, it can feel like you've lost yourself — or never even knew who you were, to begin with. Trauma doesn't make it easy, as you start to think less about exploring who you might be and the world around you and more about just surviving one day after another.

One way you can see the loss of self play out is when a codependent encounters someone new, a friend or a partner. Usually, the codependent will look into the other person's hobbies to connect with them, but the problem is knowing how far is too far. There's also the issue of never being able to tell their true interests or what they really think about certain important life issues, for instance. The codependent's sense of self comes from a role, and they often strive to be perfect at it because all of their self-worth depends on it. So, when they experience a tragedy or problem like losing a relationship or job or failing at a business endeavor, the codependent takes it harder than most. In fact, it hits so hard that they may be actively or passively suicidal, which means they may be working on a plan to take their lives, or they may just hope and wish they'd experience something fatal to put them out of their misery. Even when passive, suicide has gravity, and if you're at this point, you should reach out for professional help.

One important note about not knowing who you are is that you tend not to be aware of how things actually affect you. You may have experienced countless occasions when you accepted someone else's beliefs about you or their own version of events when your gut was telling you otherwise or suspected they were wrong. However, the thought that they could be wrong about you would make you feel terrible or sick, so you don't ask questions or challenge others. For instance, if you think a potential client should pay you better, your codependency may have you feeling it's wrong to ask for more. This makes it incredibly easy for you to be manipulated or even gaslit.

No Self-Respect

When you don't respect yourself, you feel self-loathing. This is typical of codependency. People who don't respect themselves tend to take risks when it comes to their emotions or even their health. For instance, they may have no problem getting together with someone sexually without first talking about being safe, or they may choose to risk their money by throwing it at an addict. The struggle with codependency is that it's tough to believe you're worthy. That's what makes it tough to do the safe thing instead. You get the sense that you're just not enough, that nothing you say or do or could ever be enough, and this sort of thinking is preyed upon by the media, which continues to tout perfection as an ideal to strive for.

Failure is one of the cognitive filters that can fuel the feeling of not being enough. You may be under the impression that you could never do things right. Feeling worthless and like there's something broken about you can also fan the flames of not-enoughness. Not only that, but the feeling of helplessness also makes you think you could never accomplish anything on your own and would have to depend on someone else. You get the sense that you're not even enough to care for yourself.

Desiring Approval

Have you ever felt the need to bend like a pretzel just to fit in? Do you need to act and speak in ways to get other people to like and accept you? Then that is approval-seeking behavior, typical of people pleasers. You're basically letting people know you're dealing with this issue even when you're unaware of your codependency symptoms. Others notice that you prioritize every other need and want over your own. You go so far as to anticipate what others expect and get it done to get some approval. Also, the fact that you're constantly focused on everyone and everything outside of you means you don't know what your own needs are, and that means when you think about your own interests, you feel selfish or terrible. You feel inexplicable, unjustified guilt. It's okay to feel guilty when you don't keep the promises you make yourself, and in that way, it's a good thing because it teaches you to love yourself and be someone with integrity.

However, guilt is unjustified when you feel like you need to fix things even though you're not the one who broke them. Every person on this little blue dot has their own needs and wants; therefore, it's not wrong but just part of being human. You should never feel like you are a burden, a sin, or something. If anyone treats you as if they are, they're being abusive. In healthy relationships where interdependence is the order of the day, both parties understand that the other person's perspective, thoughts, and emotions are valid, even when different from theirs. So, they meet each other halfway. The other cognitive filter you should be aware of is abandonment. When you have abandonment as a belief system, you expect that people will never be available to you, and when they are, it's only temporary because they'll leave for someone better. You may fight hard to prove you deserve to have their presence by doing all the chores at home, doing more emotional heavy lifting in the relationship than the other person, and so on.

The Inability to Negotiate

When you struggle with codependency, you find it a terrifying prospect to upset people around you. The last thing you want is to inconvenience or irritate someone, so you do everything possible to keep that from happening. Most codependents don't have self-awareness, which means they may get the sense that they've got the short end of the stick. They may be resentful, but the codependent person can't pinpoint what they need. When they realize their needs, it only makes them feel guilty, which is why they never stand up for themselves, let alone negotiate.

Codependency makes you feel like you've got to cede control of your life to others so they can be happy, and this is why you feel like you have no choice but to go along with whatever they offer. You feel you should be okay with everyone else's expectations of you, but this also makes you resent them. When you feel resentment, that emotion is trying to tell you that you've got boundaries and needs that you're not sticking up for. That may be because the concept of boundaries is completely unfamiliar to you or because you feel doing so is a shameful thing, or it scares you.

Among the debilitating schemas that CBT identifies with this struggle with negotiation are:

- Subjugation

- Emotional deprivation

- Emotional Inhibition.

Subjugation happens when you feel compelled to deny the existence of your wants, needs, and emotions because you believe others will either abandon you or fight you if you choose to express them. Emotional deprivation is trust that other people will not meet your most basic needs or that they might be able but unwilling. This is why you don't negotiate on your behalf because you get the sense that they will disappoint you again and again. Emotional inhibition is what happens when you stuff your feelings deep down inside you and don't bother to communicate because you expect people to frown or disapprove of what you're saying.

The Savior Complex

As a codependent, you're all about focusing on how you can fix others instead of looking in your own backyard. You do this to demonstrate your love and for another selfish reason, even if you're unaware of it: To have control. But the thing is, the more you try to control others, the more you feel like you're losing control because change is an intrinsic thing you can't force on someone else. Another thing to note is that your efforts at "loving" the other person will only cause them to resent you because it feels like you're trying to save them. You're telling them they need saving, and that's like saying they're incapable or inadequate.

Codependency is a struggle with denying reality, rejecting it, or downplaying the gravity of things. You may also have a penchant for assuming you know someone else better than they know themselves. So, you make assumptions about them and expect them to align with them. Or you may feel the need to save someone from their own choices. You need to realize that people will decide for themselves no matter what, and sometimes those decisions will lead to trouble. That's just life. It's not your job to dictate how their journey should go, and you're not the one to bear the responsibility for the outcomes of their actions.

One final thing to note about constantly focusing on everyone else but you is that you likely minimize or downplay your bad decisions. You have perfectly "good", and "rational" reasons for doing the same thing (or worse) than the person you're concerned about is doing. This tendency makes it tough to recover from codependency because you can only change things you accept or acknowledge about yourself. Two schemas are at play here: the undeveloped self or enmeshment and uncompromising standards. Enmeshment is when you must be fused or merged with someone else. So, you get the sense that it's fine for you to control their choices and decisions because you feel like you're doing it for both of you. As for uncompromising standards, that's fueled by the need to be perfect and a sense that there are only two ways to get things done: the right way (usually yours) and the wrong one.

Questions

Scenario: *Assume that you just got into a new business relationship with a partner. You've been meeting clients, and everything's been going great. You've got synergy. Suddenly, your partner has to bail on a meeting because of an emergency at home. Their wife is struggling with cancer, and they explain that they'll need a week off to handle things before they can resume work with you. Choose one:*

1. You get why he has to take off. But you will send them resources on alternative or experimental treatments to help him. He didn't ask you for them.

2. You understand the gravity of the situation. You can only imagine your partner and his wife's pain. You inform him that it's okay for him to show up when convenient, and if he wants to, he can call you when things clear up a bit.

3. You start off seeming like it's all good, and you get it, but then you realize you're upset because he clearly doesn't think running a business with you is that important. You also had to give up caring for loved ones to make things happen. So, you send an email telling him he shouldn't have started a business with you if he couldn't find a balance between work and marriage, and you don't feel his taking off is fair.

4. You get the sense that he may have decided he doesn't enjoy working with you or learned something about you he doesn't like, so he's ghosting on what you've built together.

Scenario: *After a lot of time and effort, you've finally saved up a certain amount of money you've always wanted to have. A couple of days later, you get a message from your family explaining that your dad got into an accident and the surgery will cost a pretty penny — pretty much all you've saved. Choose one:*

1. You gripe about how this was an unplanned spend and hope he does recover after this. You only give them half the money because you want something for yourself.

2. You straight up say you're not going to help. You get the idea that your dad's "accident" wouldn't have happened if he weren't drinking as usual. You refuse to help your dad because you'd like him to learn his lesson and improve.

3. You're ticked off because it only makes sense that right when you hit your goal, something's coming to ruin it. You give your dad the money, but you decide you'll keep in touch to ensure every cent goes towards his recovery and nothing else. You also tend to notice when he spends money on something that isn't a recovery, and you comment on that.

4. You just give him the money. He's your father, after all, and there's no better alternative.

Scenario: *You get the sense that your partner is going through something serious. You ask about it, but they tell you they don't want to discuss it. Choose one:*

1. You decide to leave them be, but it's tough for you to do that because you're worried that you're the problem.

2. You let them know you get it and are there for them. You let them know that you're there if they change their mind and want to talk about it.

3. You get upset. After all, you're their partner. You're the one person they should tell everything to. So, you let them know how you feel.

4. You get the sense that you're both done for. Your relationship is doomed if they won't tell you what's up.

Scenario: *Your wife was out all night, drinking and partying. She returns only to yell abusive things at your children, upsetting them. Choose one:*

1. You voice your opinions about her love for the bottle, and you won't let up even when she tells you that she's not going to do that again (while not telling you how she plans to keep that behavior in check).

2. You let your wife know you're aware you could never change her, but at the same time, you're not okay with her being abusive to your children. They're yours, too, and it doesn't matter that she's their mother. Her behavior is not okay, and you plan to keep them safe. You ask if she'd like to go to therapy together to fix things.

3. You choose not to speak with your wife and don't say anything to your kids either — at least, not upfront. You just do something passive-aggressive, like throwing away what's left of a bottle and acting like you didn't know it was empty.

4. You have a conversation with your children about how stressed out mommy is, and you all work out how you can do your best not to upset mom in the future when she's drunk.

Scenario: *If you're a single parent, you meet your dream person. The only issue they have is they're going to be in a state far, far away. It's more convenient for you to remain where you are. Choose one:*

1. You choose to remain where you are, but you let your parents care for your kids now and then so you can see this person. You may spend more money than you know you should going on those trips.

2. You understand the importance of stability for your children, so you refuse to disrupt things by leaving. You decide to keep seeing this person and see if it's working out in 6 months to a year.

3. You remain with your children, but you never stop beating them over the head with all the things you're giving up just to take care of them when they do something that drives you up the wall.

4. You realize that if you don't move with this person, someone else will take your place in his life. They're the best person,

and you need to do everything possible to make things work. So, you let your parents worry about the kids while you move in with them.

Scenario: *After so much pain and heartbreak, you finally find it in you to end your relationship with a toxic person. But then, they send you a message saying they'd like to meet. Choose one:*

1. You're excited, so you agree to meet. You reflect on your response and remember all the reasons this relationship was doomed from the start. So, you send them another message to cancel them.

2. You let them know you believe they deserve good things in life, but you have no desire to be one of those things. You tell them never to call or message again.

3. You see the message, but you choose not to respond. You know that would irk the person because you've gained the advantage.

4. You should at least hear them out, so you go to see them. They let you know things will be different this time because they've been working on themselves (the same spiel they've given you countless times, even though nothing really changed). You decide you'll give things another go, and anyone who doesn't like it can mind their own business.

Scenario: *Money has gone missing from the joint account you have with your partner. You ask him about it, and he says he's been* *trading cryptocurrencies with it. He just needs to hit a good run of luck, and he'll have the money back and then some. Choose one:*

1. Tell him you get his attempts to make back the money, but it's not wise to risk any more of your money. To help prevent that, you're going to revoke his access to the account at the bank.

2. You ask him when his gambling addiction began and if he'd like to see professional help to stop. If he doesn't want to, you decide you'll talk to an attorney about how to keep your money safe without ending your marriage.

3. You let him know you expected no less than betrayal from him, just like other people have betrayed you in the past.

4. You're okay with him trying to make back the money. You'll do this because, after all, he doesn't give you much flack about your own faults.

Scenario: *Things have been tough lately. Your boss is upset with you, your kids are upset with you, and on top of that, you've had to battle traffic for three hours only to get home and find a bill that hasn't been paid and will cost a fair bit more than you had planned to spend for the month. Choose one:*

1. You feel bad for a bit, turn on the TV, drink and eat a bit too much, vent to a good friend, then get it together, shower, and hit the sack.

2. It occurs to you that struggles are part of the human experience, and while this day was bad, that doesn't mean the previous ones have been, or future ones will be as bad. So, you find healthy ways to cope (like yoga, perhaps), which calms you.

3. You think about how your supervisor embarrassed you and sent him a strongly worded email.

4. You think you're a failure. That's the only thing you can think.

Scenario: *You have a good friend who continues to cancel plans at the last minute and is never there when you're emotionally stressed. Some other friend says something about this, and it hurts. Choose one:*

1. You see the truth in their words, but you're not sure how to discuss it with this flak friend the next time you meet if she finally doesn't cancel.

2. You let the friend who pointed out the other person's flakiness know that you appreciate them for bringing that up, as you've found it problematic. You tell them you'll discuss things with your flaky friend, and you do that. You let this flaky person know what you need from them, and after that, you watch to see if they respect your needs more or if things remain the same. If the latter is the case, you do what's best for you.

3. You tell this mutual friend you don't mind that she's flaky. After all, you have the hots for your significant other.

4. Your mutual friend is wrong, and you let her know that. It's fine for your friend to be as she is because there's much on her plate. Besides, you see her once in a while, and considering how busy she is, it's nice that she does that.

Scenario: *You've been stoked about an end-of-year party for months as you see friends and family you haven't been with throughout the year. On your way, your wife sends a message saying she needs you at home, so she doesn't begin cutting again. Choose one:*

1. You've waited forever for this party, so you choose to go. You don't have any intention of disappointing friends and family. You compromise with your wife by offering to call every half hour to check-in.

2. You empathize with your wife and let her know you know things are tough right now. However, you've made a commitment. You tell her to reach out to a friend nearby and to keep in mind that you're not responsible for her choices.

3. You turn the car around and head home. You hate that you're going back. You're mean to her until you both turn in for the night.

4. You head back home because it's absolutely not okay to be selfish in this situation.

Results

1s: Getting mostly 1s means you're not heavily codependent or you've been working on yourself and making progress. However, you need to know what you need, be more assertive, and let others handle their issues. You'll learn how later.

2s: Getting this means you're interdependent. If you were codependent before, you've recovered. You'll still find the exercises in this workbook useful because there's no reason you shouldn't learn to do better than you are.

3s: You're dealing with codependency consistently. You tend to be passive-aggressive, which means your needs go unmet because no one knows you have them. You interpret their ignorance as them deliberately hurting you, and you hurt them back indirectly, even though they have no clue they've hurt you. You'll learn about automatic thoughts that cause you to act this way in a later chapter. You deserve to have your needs and to voice them, and you should also know that just because you make them known doesn't mean people will be able to meet them. You can be more assertive and more accepting of "no." You'll see.

4s: You're dealing with codependency fueled by low self-worth and inadequacy. So, you want to fix things by being of service to everyone. However, you only have so much in terms of resources. You're eventually going to run dry, and when that happens, you'll wind up full of resentment, leading to automatic thoughts that make you feel inferior to everyone else when you aren't. You're worthy. The trouble is that you encourage others to take advantage of you.

Before moving on to the second part of this book, note that codependency is a detachment from the authentic self, so as you begin with the exercises, you're naturally not going to be certain about your needs, values, identity, beliefs, and so on. You'll learn how to find yourself, and in that lies true power. You'll come to trust yourself, care for yourself more, and finally, love the person you see in the mirror.

Chapter 3

Goals for Successful Recovery

In this chapter, you'll learn the importance of developing self-awareness, which will help you break free from codependence and truly love yourself. You need to learn to love who you really are before you can give love to anyone else, and that begins with having a relationship with yourself. As you develop this relationship, you will naturally learn more about yourself and start to feel connected to the core of who you really are. This means that one day, you can truly say you know who you are.

Why Set Goals?

Think about why you decided to do something about your codependency; when you know your why, you'll be more committed to successfully breaking free and know the goals you need to set for yourself. When you set goals, you can tell who you really are, and the process can help you heal your wounds. Goals help you figure out where you're going and the best way to get there, which means that without them, you'd be lost. Goals also let you know what matters most, and they come to you intuitively. The question is, what's keeping you from making them happen? You may feel insecure and afraid of criticism and failure.

If you're going to set goals, they have to be specific before you can accomplish them. If your goals are vague, it's easy to have results you don't like. For instance, if you'd like to address your cigarette addiction, you may decide to cut down on how many sticks you smoke without looking into the actual reason you smoke. Maybe you smoke when you feel stressed and depressed. Then you may decide to replace this addiction with something healthier in your mind, like going to the gym. Sure, it seems like it's a healthy choice, but you may find yourself going a little longer and harder than you should.

You need specific goals. You need to be clear about your intentions to change and make proper assessments of where you're at. It's not enough to tell yourself, "I'll do better." If your goal is to hit the gym, it's more specific to think of lifting more weight with time rather than just saying you want to increase your strength. If your goal is specific, you'll see yourself taking steps to make it real for you, motivating you to keep going. If you want to be strong, you may go to the gym but never lift heavier because there's no specific goal in mind, and as a result, you'll never know how strong you can get.

Benefits of Goal Setting

Goals help to keep you going when times get tough because they inspire you to succeed: Sometimes, we need a little push. If we are having a hard time, we find an event or circumstance that can inspire us to succeed. Whether it's a loss in a competition or an unexpected financial setback, goals help us face adversity and challenge. If you want to feel like you're making progress against your personal goals, ask yourself: "If I didn't have this goal, what will keep me going?" In other words, think about the benefits of achieving your goal before you start chasing it.

Goals provide direction and motivation, keeping you focused on the most important tasks and removing distractions: Life is full of distractions, and it's almost impossible to do everything we want to do. Achieving goals is a good solution to this problem. Having goals helps you focus on what matters and eliminate distractions so you can get your work done and enjoy life more.

Goals help us plan for the future: If a goal is not set, it may not be clear where we are going or how we will get there. Remember that this process is your personal journey and one that you can change or stop at any time if necessary. An important part of making progress toward your goals is seeing where you're going so that you'll know what to do next.

Goals help to measure your efforts and whether or not you are successful: Goal setting is not just about working toward the future. It is also a way to check your progress. If we don't know the distance between where we are and where we want to go, it's hard to appreciate our achievements or notice our mistakes. After all, it's hard to tell if you're moving forward if you don't know where your starting point was in the first place!

Goals provide a balance in life: Many of us live constantly imbalanced lives, often putting work ahead of pleasure and relationships. While this is understandable, goals make it clear when we are out of balance and show us how to get back on track.

Goals encourage a sense of urgency for action, which results in better decision-making: When we don't have to decide what to do next or whether or not we will get something done, many of us simply procrastinate. Sooner or later, the task that isn't completed gets in our way, causing stress and panic. However, if you have a future goal, you are forced to face the consequences of your action or inaction. Therefore, it is much easier to decide what comes first because you know exactly how it will affect other things you want to do.

Goals allow you to maintain a positive attitude because they are always being worked towards: When we have goals to work toward, it is very easy to remain committed and optimistic. There is something that motivates us to achieve our goals, which keeps us going even when we might be discouraged by the process itself.

Goals make you feel good: When you have a goal, it's easy to feel good about yourself because you can look at progress and measure your achievements against what you thought was possible. We feel proud when we meet or exceed expectations, and this sense of accomplishment keeps us motivated.

Short Term Targets

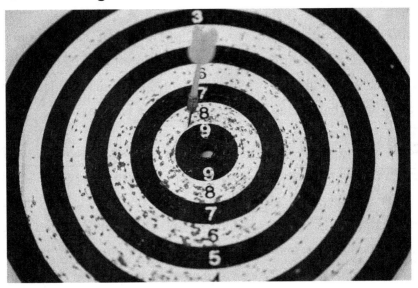

When it comes to goals, is often a tendency to look at the big picture instead. For instance, you know you need to come to a place where you start saying no. You realize the importance of being in healthy relationships. These are the things that make you very happy in life. However, you must remember that to get the bigger picture, you must consider short-term goals. Short-term goals are the goals that you can make happen in less than a year. These goals together make up the big long-term goal you would like to make a reality. Assume, for instance, that you desire to have published a book. This would be considered a long-term goal. That goal can be further broken down into many short-term goals, such as figuring out your table of contents, what each chapter will entail, and so on. There is a lot of power in setting short-term goals because when you have them clearly mapped out, you will find that your big, seemingly unrealistic dreams are easy to attain in your mind. The other wonderful thing about having short-term goals is that as you cross each one off your list, you will subconsciously realize that you are very capable and that there is nothing you can't accomplish. Naturally, this realization will give you all the drive and motivation you need.

Long Term Targets

Think of your long-term targets as the dreams that you have. These are the things that would give you the most joy in life. One good goal to have for the long term is to come to a place where you love and accept yourself fully. It is impossible to attain these goals because they seem too big and too grand. However, when you break them down into smaller tasks, you will find these goals very attainable.

Remember, when it comes to changing your life to attain your dreams, you may not notice the changes initially. Say, for instance, you would like to come to a place where you can forgive your partner for all the pain they've caused you. It may not seem as though you are progressing forward, but if you make sure you've got small goals that lead to the bigger ones, you'll find yourself doing well. Some of the smaller goals you can set for yourself include being more compassionate towards yourself, working on your trauma with a licensed professional therapist, or writing in your journal to your loved one about how you really feel. With time, you will eventually find it within yourself to forgive your partner. All you have to do is commit to the smaller goals that lead to the large ones.

Starting Now

If you're ready to take control of your life, you first have to consider what you want to achieve. Where do you want to steer your life to? Think about what it would feel like when you were self-actualized and how you would be. It would be helpful for you to do this exercise with a journal. Write about the best version of yourself that you can imagine. Contemplate how you would look and act at work, in your relationships, in friendships, and so on. You may want to be financially free or to come to a place where you are aware of your boundaries and enforce them. The best version of yourself is surrounded by people who are good for you. If you are struggling with some addiction, the best version of yourself may have found a healthy way to deal with it. They definitely would have stopped submitting and succumbing to the power of whatever substance has them hooked. As you contemplate and write about your best self, do not think there is anything too lofty or too high a goal to attain. Go as big as you can and be as reckless with your imagination as a child who hasn't heard the word " no " or understood the concept of rejection.

The first step: What worries you? Write it all down.

Now it's time to dive deep into what you find concerning. What about your life has got you feeling so heavy and low? What is it you find most disheartening about your condition of codependency and the likelihood of you recovering from that? Be honest with yourself as you write.

Cue 1: *As you journaled about the best version of yourself, you were able to notice certain obstacles, which include:*

_____

_____

_____

(Some examples of obstacles are money, energy, time, health, not enough education, etc.)

Cue 2: *Sometimes, in the process of wanting to make something good happen, we get frightened of the consequences that are sure to come as a result of the changes that we make. For instance, deciding that you would like to have much better people around you could mean losing the friends that you do have. If you can finally recover from your codependency, think about at least one thing you are afraid of that will change. If there's more than one thing, go ahead and write them all down.*

_____

_____

_____

Cue 3: *Take a moment to think about what it would be like to have someone's unconditional support. What sort of advice would you offer if you were to tell them about the obstacles you're facing in cue 1? What fresh perspectives might they have that you're not able to* *see? How might they encourage you to get through the fears that you are faced with?*

_____

_____

_____

The second step: Setting Goals

Remember, you must set goals for both the short term and the long term to have an effective total recovery. In this part of the exercise, it's time to contemplate what those goals mean to you.

Cue 1: *For the long term, these are the three things that I would most love to change about my life:*

_____

_____

_____

Cue 2: *Now it's time to think about three smaller short-term goals you could focus on for each of the long-term goals you listed in Cue 2. For instance, you can develop a bunch of healthy friendships in the long run. Some of the short-term goals could look like this:*

1. Get some therapy to help me deal with my anxiety around people.

2. Actively seek out meetup groups or classes that revolve around my interests.

3. Say yes to any invitation I get, or participate in work events and network more.

_____

_____

_____

Cue 3: *For each of the short-term goals you have figured out in Cue 2, think about an even shorter-term goal that you can easily knock out of the park in a matter of a week.* For instance, your long-term goal may be to develop better and new friendships. Your short-term goal to make that happen could mean accepting invitations to various events. An even shorter-term goal to make that previous goal happen could be changing your wardrobe because you realize it makes you feel uncomfortable. After all, you have nothing good to wear in your mind. You could decide that you'll buy five new tops and five new bottoms this week.

When You Slip Up

No one is perfect, so it's natural to expect that you will make a mistake as you try to accomplish your goals. Because you're struggling with codependency, the odds are you also have quite the streak of perfectionism in you. You can take advantage of this perfectionism by also making plans for your mistakes because you will make them. Make no mistake about that. Everyone who's ever tried to attain a goal every now and then can feel themselves slipping. This is only natural. The important thing you need to remember is that you can pick up right where you left off. You are not a terrible person or a disappointment for slipping up. In fact, the very process of slipping up can be very beneficial. As you make mistakes, think about what the mistakes tell you about what you think, how you've been acting, and the situation that added to your mistake or loss of motivation. Just because you slipped up does not mean you failed. Therefore, when you make mistakes, you should observe the thought processes in your mind that may not be fruitful or motivate you to get back up and at it. The information in the next chapter will teach you how to think correctly to ensure your recovery.

Chapter 4

Distortions in Your Head

Spotting Negative Thoughts

The thing about mental health disorders is that having them tends to lead to automatic thought processes that are usually negative. Sometimes the thoughts are visual, and other times they're verbal. For instance, you may envision a ceiling fan falling and crashing over someone's head. Or you may have thoughts that are simply hateful words. The thing about these negative thoughts is that there is not an iota of truth to them. They take the reality of the situation and color it differently. And not only that, but they also cause you to react in a way that is not beneficial to you or the other person involved. You're about to discover ten of the most popular cognitive distortions you can learn. Identify them whenever you are experiencing them, and you can put the kibosh on them.

1. **All-or-nothing:** This thought process involves thinking of things only in extremes. It doesn't matter whether you're thinking about yourself, your situation, or someone else. It will always be either one thing or the other, and both are often on the extreme ends of a spectrum. For instance, you may assume that you are a total and complete failure just because you're making a mistake and one aspect of your life. However, that may not be true. You may be in the middle of your learning curve and haven't quite hit your stride yet. If you want to find out if you are engaged in all-or-nothing thinking, you must pay attention when the words "never" or "always" pop up. It is often the case that neither of those words is true. You may be able to identify this particular sentiment: "I always show up for others, but they never show up for me."

2. **Mental filtering**: When it comes to mental filtering, you never consider the big picture. Your mind is solely focused on everything negative about someone or some situation you're dealing with, which only causes you to feel even more stressed. For instance, you may say and think that you had a terrible day, but in reality, you only paid attention to the things that went wrong, far less than everything else that went right for you that day. It's not the same thing as minimizing the positives because when it comes to mental filtering, you don't see anything good.

3. **Disregarding or minimizing the positive:** Also known as the Fortune telling error, this cognitive distortion is what you experience when you feel like you're able to tell what the future holds. However, your prediction is a terrible one. When it comes to how you're going to handle the negative situation if it ever occurs, you tend to exaggerate. Because you're brewing a storm in a teacup, you inevitably feel more anxious, and this can lead you to procrastinate, avoid things you should do, or simply remain passive about things you should take action on. This is also known as catastrophizing, and one of the ways you can do that is by thinking, for instance, "It's not okay for me to let others know my true feelings, or they will hate me and ridicule me. My life will be totally ruined if that happens."

4. **Emotional reasoning:** When dealing with emotional reasoning, you assume that something you feel must be true. Otherwise, you wouldn't feel it, would you? The reality of the situation is that people's emotions are subjective. This

implies that not everyone feels the same about everything. For instance, you may think about a certain coworker and get the feeling that they don't like you, so your feeling must be true. In fact, it's quite possible that many people actually love you. But because you are dealing with emotional reasoning, you tend to interpret your interactions with these people through the assumptions that you're feelings inspire.

5. **Overgeneralizing**: This cognitive distortion happens when you come to a conclusion that is not only overly dramatic but cynical and beyond the scope of what's really going on in the moment. For instance, you may think you'll never find love when you just walk out on a bad date.

6. **Mind reading**: Codependent people tend to assume that they know everything someone else thinks and feels. It never occurs to them once that they may not be right in their assumptions. It also never enters their minds that there may be other options or that they could simply ask the other person what's going on with them. Often, not only are their assumptions not correct but there are also negative ones. For instance, you may assume that your partner doesn't really care about you because they're not acting in a way you think they should in response to something you just told them. It doesn't enter your mind that they may simply be processing what you've just told them about.

7. **Personalizing**: This distortion and thought happens when you take responsibility for things that are not your problem. For instance, erroneously assume that you are the reason

someone else is feeling bad, even when other causes could fuel their mood. Say you have a significant other who hasn't called you all day. You may think that you probably did or said something to tick them off, but that's not necessarily the case. Whenever you make things personal or take responsibility for those things you shouldn't, you tend to ignore the other causes of the situation you're looking at. What if your partner is simply tired and wants to take a nap? What if your partners had a long day and were angry because they disagreed with a colleague? What if they're not feeling their best and don't want to put that on you?

8. **Labeling:** With labeling, you appoint yourself as a critical judge over yourself or someone else for some trait or event. Your court decision can be very extreme, and when you label your own self, it causes you to feel even more shame than you already do. For instance, if you're attempting a new career as a trader, you continue to lose time and time again. You may assume that you are a dumb, unintelligent person when really what's going on is that you are just still learning the craft, or you are not cut out for that particular line of work, and that's all. When you decide to label other people, it makes it impossible for you to understand who they really are. For instance, you may assume that just because your friend wants to take some space away from you to come back later because of a heated argument, they're being mean to you when that's not the case. Your friend may simply decide they don't want to make the situation any worse than it is, so they want to cool off before they can come back and discuss it with you.

9. **"Should" or "must" statements:** When you're affected by this cognitive distortion, you tend to have an expectation that is very rigid when it comes to how you or other people should behave. You also tend to blow up how terrible it could be if these expectations aren't followed. For instance, you may believe that it is important for your partner to always be on call for you to feel like they love you. Since your partner most definitely has other things going on in their life, this obviously is not true and not feasible. So, when they have to attend to the other important aspects of their life, they wind up feeling like they've been abandoned.

The trouble with these cognitive distortions is that they tend to make us see ourselves, other people, and our lives in ways that do not benefit us and always lead to more stress and suffering. These distortions and thoughts tend to make you feel terrible, and you act based on your feelings, and as a result, your actions are hardly ever beneficial. They do nothing good for you or your relationships with others. As a result of these cognitive distortions, you may have chosen to start fights with people or refuse to let them know clearly and plainly what you need from them. As a result of how you handle things, you tend to feed the fire of these cognitive distortions even more, leading to a cycle that you feel completely hopeless about and unable to break free from. One thing you should note about codependency is that it's not easy to figure out your emotions, and you may not have the words to name them. So, you'll learn the basic emotions that can help you with the exercise.

- Anger is synonymous with frustration, irritation, and annoyance.

- Sadness involves disappointment and despair. Grief can also play a part in sadness.

- Happiness involves feeling joy.

- Shame is about embarrassment, worthlessness, and inadequacy.

- Guilt often goes hand in hand with shame.

- Stress and distress often accompany each other.

- Calm involves acceptance and peace.

Other emotions include hope, gratitude, passion, excitement, loving and being loved, and so on.

Exercise 1

Assume you and your partner are attending an event together at your friend's home. Your partner lets you know that they intend to relax as much as possible because they've had a tough day at work, so they are planning to have some drinks before you head out. Take a look at your thoughts and how they could affect how you feel and act.

Assumption 1: *This is just perfect. Now I will have to babysit my partner instead of having a good time. I know they will embarrass me if I don't keep an eye on them.*

Emotions: Worry. Anxiety. Resentment. Anger.

Actions: Following a partner around all night so you can keep an eye on how many drinks they've had. Adding water to his drink whenever he leaves the table to go to the bathroom. Not being able to pay attention whenever your friends come around to have a conversation because you're too busy observing your partner.

Assumption 2: *Why do they need to have a bottle to make them feel good? Aren't I more than enough to help them feel relaxed and at ease?*

Emotions: Anger. Hurt. Shame.

Actions: Bottling up how you feel while they drink. Feel shame and embarrassment about how your partner relates or interacts with friends better than with you. Being passive-aggressive is you talk about your friends and their relationships being better than yours.

Assumption 3: *I really don't like the fact that they're going to be drunk before we get there, but there's nothing I can do about that, so I'm just going to keep my mind on my friends tonight instead of thinking about what my partner might do wrong.*

Emotions: Disappointment. Acceptance. Calm.

Actions: You take a moment to steady yourself. You make peace with the fact that your partner can do whatever they want. You decide to have a good time with your friends yourself instead of tailing your partner all through the night.

Now think about the possible outcomes in terms of emotions and actions for future scenarios. You can write about the responses in your journal or in the space provided for each assumption.

_____

_____

_____

Exercise 2

All the family's financial responsibilities fell to you when your father passed on. Your mother married another husband, who eventually left her for someone else. Since he left, she has called you several times daily and has shown up at your house without letting you know. You feel obligated to make sure you're available to meet her needs, causing poor performance at work because you're mentally and physically exhausted. She calls you and asks you to come to see her on a particularly rough night.

Assumption 1: _I don't have a choice. I'd better just head over there anyway. Since I'm the only one my mother can turn to, I really don't have a choice but to go see her._

Emotions:

_____

_____

_____

Actions:

_____

_____

_____

Assumption 2: *That woman is simply too needy. I mean, I get it; she's heartbroken. But can she just take care of herself for once?*

Emotions:

_____

_____

_____

Actions:

_____

_____

_____

Exercise 3

You just got engaged. Your best friend seems happy for you, except you've noticed that they're starting to flirt with your partner hardcore. Even worse, your partner is not only not discouraging it but doesn't seem to mind either. You want to talk to your best friend about this problem, but the following are the assumptions and thoughts you're having:

Assumption 1: *Wait a minute. I imagine there's more there than there is. I mean, they're both friends too. I'd like them to be close. Why should I feel some type of way about that?*

Emotions:

_____

_____

_____

Actions:

_____

_____

_____

Assumption 2: *The last thing I want to do is cause any issues or a rift between us. I should say nothing about it. I will do my best to keep my partner's attention at home by dressing sexier, being more passionate, and doing anything else I can do.*

Emotions:

_____

_____

_____

Actions:

_____

_____

_____

Now it's time to think about the situations you're dealing with that make you automatically assume negative things. Pick a situation bugging you, and then use the following format.

1.   *What's the situation you're dealing with?*

_____

_____

_____

2. *What thoughts have you had about this? Do your best to spot the distortions in thinking.*

_____

_____

_____

3. *What are the emotions you feel when you think of those negative thoughts?*

_____

_____

_____

4. *How have you acted, or how are you tempted to react on account of the emotions you feel?*

_____

_____

_____

5. *How do your actions affect your relationships and the way you see yourself?*

_____

_____

_____

Facing Your Negative Thoughts

Now you can see the errors in thinking that you're prone to, it's time to challenge them. To do so, you have to catch them. The good news is there isn't a negative thought you can't challenge, and doing so will cause you to feel more at ease.

Cognitive Restructuring: Begin by noticing when you have strong emotions, as this could signal that you're thinking automatically and overexaggerating your feelings. Pause and unpack the thoughts that are being fueled by the emotions. Then you can challenge them through a process known as cognitive restructuring, which involves arguing with irrational thoughts to prove their irrationality and replace them with rational ones. How do you know the difference? Rational beliefs tend to empower you, while irrational beliefs cause you to defeat yourself.

Seek Evidence: To challenge your beliefs, you have to think about the event or situation that caused the distortion in your thoughts. For instance, you could ask yourself for the evidence you're looking at that supports the distorted thought. You'll likely find it doesn't exist or doesn't make sense.

Pragmatic Questioning: Another way is to think about the consequences of not releasing the distorted thought using pragmatic questioning. For instance, ask yourself what you think your life would be like years down the road if you continue to abdicate your will to others and never assert yourself because you think others will reject you. Thinking this way means you'll never communicate your needs clearly and directly, so they'll never be met, which means you'll be resentful.

Move from absolute thinking to stating preferences: You can shift from thinking in extremes to simply considering your preferences, and in the process, you'll find yourself dealing with disappointment much better than ever. For instance, you could tell yourself, "My preference would be never to be rejected by anyone. However, I know this is impossible; therefore, I can simply learn to handle rejection like a champ. This way, I can be true to myself."

Note that it's possible to have at least three and at most all cognitive distortions before you begin the process of cognitive restructuring. This is nothing to be ashamed of because it's a natural byproduct of codependency. Don't judge yourself. You should be proud that you're aware of them now, as that means you're well on the road to recovery. The distortions in thought are things you developed from experiences you had as a child that demanded you come up with them so you can cope better. Now, you're grown, and there's no need for that. Noticing the distortions is a clear sign that you're doing better already. Here are some examples of cognitive restructuring in action, so you can put it to use in your life.

Exercise 1

Imagine your partner sends you a text where they blame you for their bad day because you cut their sleep short by accidentally dropping something. Naturally, you're upset and overwhelmed by this message from them. You now believe your whole day is ruined thanks to this text message.

Challenge 1 — Reality Check: Consider the evidence supporting your assumption, if it even exists.

Okay, pump the brakes. What's the evidence that my partner's anger means my whole day is a disaster? I know she feels angry, and so do I. This text has me feeling defensive. However, I cannot control how she feels. For my part, it's still possible for me to have a good day. I'm at work, not with her, so I can make my day as nice as I'd like. Once I'm in a good mood, I can speak with her to smooth things over before I get home.

Challenge 2 — Pragmatic Questioning: Consider the consequences you'd have to contend with if you continue this negative line of thought.

This text has me thinking the whole day is now a disaster, but if I keep thinking this, it will definitely be a disaster. I won't be able to help myself because I'll be stuck feeling angry, defensive, and worried about what it'll be like when I get back home to my partner. I'll have a miserable day, and if I keep reacting to things like this in the same manner, I may never find healthy ways to handle life's challenges.

Challenge 3 — Proper Perspective: Put things in proper perspective. Understand that your preferences aren't absolutes, and there are always alternatives.

While I would prefer my partner not to be upset with me, and I know that she shouldn't be upset with me for making an honest mistake, I realize things don't have to be how I'd prefer them. I'd like us to have a good time tonight, but I know I cannot control that. I can at least have a good day.

Exercise 2

Now it's time to look at situations in your life that you can use cognitive restructuring on. Write out the situation in a journal first, and then note your thoughts and feelings on the matter. When you're done, apply the three challenges in the same format as the sample exercise you've been given. Do this for as many situations as you desire, and keep practicing these challenges as things arise that cause negative thoughts.

Replacing the Negative Thoughts

Now that you've acknowledged and challenged them, it's time to replace them. You can do this because, thanks to your shift in perspective, you can see other viable options to your problem than the absolutes you arrive at. The new thoughts should support you more because you're working on the reality of your situation, which means you won't feel as overwhelmed as you used to. You will feel empowered. A good coping skill is looking for and implementing supportive thoughts instead of negative ones. You recover better, faster, and stronger each time you pull that off.

Let's go back to cognitive distortions. Each one has a positive, supportive thought that matches it. For instance, when you tend to downplay the positive in your life, you can remind yourself it's only natural for both good things and bad things to happen, and it's fine to give them equal weight, or if you can swing it, to focus more on celebrating the good.

Exploring the Evidence: This is a good strategy to replace negative thoughts. For instance, you may assume, "I'm such a lazy person for scaling back on work and taking time off to focus on me." When you dive deeper into this belief, it may occur to you that every time you've seen others model self-care in this way, you've felt nothing but respect for them. You may also have seen that they're not as stressed as you and get much more accomplished. So, you could replace your original thought with this one: "Sure, I feel lazy about taking time off for me, but I can always teach myself to cope with that feeling and that it's actually productive to do so."

Note that as you explore the evidence, your original thought may have some truth to it. That doesn't mean you cannot replace that truth with something that's a more positive thought because you need to remember that everything in life is on a spectrum. Sure, some people get upset with you for setting boundaries, but it doesn't mean every person in your life will reject you for being clear about them. In fact, you could remind yourself, "There are those who will respect me all the more for being clear about my boundaries. While having people be upset with me is uncomfortable, I still have to be clear about my limits and needs so that I don't harbor resentment.

If you struggle with replacing negative thoughts with positive ones, try putting someone else in your position. Imagine they're thinking the same negative thought that plagues you, and you just might be able to see the reality of the situation better by putting some distance between you and the thought this way. The more you practice, the less you'll think negatively. Eventually, that will stop. However, this isn't going to happen overnight, so be patient and give yourself grace. Mindfulness will help you with this, and you'll learn more about it in another chapter. The following is an example you can use to replace negative thoughts.

Exercise 3

You're about to invite some friends to your birthday party, and you start to feel bad. You think it won't go well. People will be late, some of your friends might not get along with others, and this could cause drama. You're no longer excited about the party because you're certain it will be a disappointment. How can you replace this thought process?

Step 1 — Recognition: First, notice you now have negative thoughts.

> *I can see I'm worried that my birthday party will be terrible. This will make me feel miserable for days. I'm clearly overgeneralizing and making things out to be a catastrophe.*

Step 2 — Respecting Emotions: Notice your feelings, and then use the previously mentioned cognitive restructuring exercise.

> *It's okay to feel nervous. My birthday is clearly important. I can't do anything to control my friends, but I do know they've always been there for me and have shown me support. Sure, some of them may not be able to get along with each other, but I'm sure they care enough about me to at least be civil. Also, if I keep thinking things will be a disaster, I'll probably find myself pressuring them to act right, and that's not fair.*

Step 3 — Replacing the Thoughts: Work with the thoughts you've identified in the second step to create a new way of looking at things that offer more balance in perspective.

> *So, I'm concerned about my birthday party not going well because some of my friends don't get along. However, even if the worst thing happens, like a dramatic fight, that doesn't*

mean my friends will love me any less. It's just one party. It changes nothing about my friendships.

Now it's time for you to do the same thing with your own negative thoughts. Use the prompts from the sample exercise to help you. You may do this in your journal or down below:

_____

_____

_____

Chapter 5

Feeling Triggered?

Many codependents find themselves anxious about their thoughts, worried that they may not be accepted, and concerned that they aren't as they'd like. This chapter is meant to help you address your triggers, which are the situations that lead you to feel anxious. To heal, you need to address your triggers. If this makes you feel afraid, it's natural, but you can't avoid it. Acting like they don't exist is only effective until your triggers confront you again. So, it's time to face your fears so that you can reduce them and the impact of fear itself on your life.

Before we get into fear, it's important to consider the difference between the triggers discussed here and traumatic triggers. The latter is the sort that happens on account of specific smells, sensations, sounds, things, and situations that could remind your brain and body of something traumatic you went through. For instance, if you were physically abused as a kid by someone who drank a lot, you may feel uncomfortable or anxious whenever you smell or see alcohol. You know you're dealing with a traumatic trigger when you get the sense that you're dissociating. Dissociation happens when you feel like your mind is in a fog or you're floating or not in your body. If it's not dissociation, it could be a panic attack. If these are the triggers you're dealing with, you should get help from a trauma therapist. You can use exposure therapy (which you'll learn about in a moment), but it's best to get help.

The Root of All Fear

Your amygdala is where the feeling of fear begins, activating your fight-fight-freeze-fawn response to keep you safe from the threats you're faced with, whether real or perceived. When you feel fear, certain physiological effects help you pick the best of the four responses that work for the situation at hand or for you. For instance, say you're faced with a tiger. Your prefrontal cortex and hippocampus make it possible to see if you're dealing with a dangerous situation because just because something seems threatening doesn't mean it really is.

Exposure Therapy: One of the best ways to deal with your fear is through exposure therapy, which is not something that happens just once as it's a process. The first thing you need to do is think about the things that trigger your anxiety. Some of the situations that could be a problem include having to set boundaries, making new friends, or even having to go for a run. Maybe you'd like to go running to get fitter, but you tend to be self-critical because you feel you're overweight and look weird to everyone for running. You could try little things like running only within your neighborhood, going with good friends and family who support you, joining inclusive gyms, and so on. You can then gauge your anxiety levels as you complete each. Assessing yourself will show you you're more than capable of dealing with your anxiety and even defeating it.

Response Prevention: Knowing your triggers allows you to learn to react differently by considering other reactions besides your typical, automatic ones. Response prevention is about developing effective plans to deal with your trigger the next time you face it and committing to acting on your plan when it's time.

Example of Exposure Therapy in Action

Let's assume that ever since you and your partner have been together, you've always had to handle everything to do with the house. You realize from day one; your partner would always ask you what dinner was and never even tried to help you make the meals or clean up. You didn't have a problem with it at first because you thought you'd find yourself a catch and thought they were better than you. The last thing you want is to give them any reason to walk out on you. However, you've become resentful of them over time. You see, you don't earn as much as they do, and so in your mind, you think you owe your partner cooked meals and a clean house. However, you now want to go after your own interests, which means you'll need more time, energy, and resources. So, you need to discuss with your partner about sharing household tasks, but thinking of doing that makes you apprehensive and scared. Here's how you could practice exposure therapy.

Step 1: *You craft a list of all the ways you can convince and challenge yourself to say something on your own behalf, which makes it possible for you to move towards speaking with your partner. Here are some ideas:*

- I have to tell my coworker that I will no longer let them keep passing their work on to me.

- I have to tell my dad that he can't just come to my house without calling.

- I will write down what I'm going to say to my partner and then rehearse it till it feels natural. Then I'll roleplay talking to my partner with a friend.

- The next time the neighbor's kid breaks one of my potted plants, I will ask them to pay for it instead of telling them it's all right.

Step 2: *You could assess the level of anxiety you expect to have when you decide to do each of these things, measuring from a scale of 0 to 10, with 0 meaning no anxiety and 10 being the most anxious you could be. You will also take your time to think about the different outcomes you might get due to these actions.*

- My coworker may like me less for not wanting to do his work for him, but that's his problem, not mine. Anxiety level: 5.

- My dad has a famously terrible temper. I'm not looking forward to that, but I have to get it over with because I'm done letting him be a tyrant in my life. Anxiety level: 7.

- This person is my friend, and I'm sure they love and support me. So, they'll let me roleplay. Who knows, they could also offer me helpful tips. I still feel anxious doing this because I don't know how my partner will react. Anxiety level: 2.

- My neighbor may not care that I'm putting my foot down about his child destroying my property, but on the upside, she'll have to do something to keep that from happening again, so she doesn't have to keep paying me. Still, I'd have to see her around most days, but I can work on ignoring her or not feeling guilty. Anxiety level: 6.

Step 3: *With time, you'll assert yourself by deliberately exposing yourself to triggers so that your anxiety can lessen significantly, enough to make you desensitized. This will help you speak to your partner about your issues, and then you can assess whether your predictions about their reaction are accurate. If there's anything that isn't true, you can cancel it, and you'll learn that your predictions are negative and inaccurate. This will make you even less fearful about stating your needs and asserting yourself in the future.*

Exercise for Triggers

Now it's your turn to implement the above. Think about the people and circumstances that trigger your anxiety. Think about everything and everyone you've kept a distance from because you're afraid. For instance, does public speaking terrify you? Are you worried about setting boundaries for your kid? Figure out what the trigger is, and then do this exercise.

Step 1: *Write in your journal about the situation or person that makes you anxious and what you want to experience instead. Also, think about at least three things you can do that will help you work your way up to the larger goal.*

_____

_____

_____

72

Step 2: *Think about your expectations of how things will play out before you do each of the three things you've assigned yourself, and rate the level of anxiety you think you'll experience as you confront each situation on a scale of 0 to 10. Remember, 0 is no anxiety, and 10 is the most anxiety you've ever felt.*

Step 3: *Go over what actually happened and cancel any predictions you made that didn't happen.*

Response Prevention Plan Exercise

Assume for a moment that you have a partner who has cheated on you several times and claims each time that he's going to do better and stop. Each time you think about how he's been unfaithful, it feels like you're being torn apart, and life means nothing to you. You're overcome with morbid, depressing thoughts and have even had to be hospitalized because of your suicidal ideation. Once, you even physically attacked your partner, but no one knew about this, and he thought he deserved it. You carry a lot of hope that he will not be unfaithful to you anymore, but you know that it's important to have a response in place in case it happens again.

Your Response Prevention Plan

Step 1: Think about the triggers for this situation.

Some triggers may include discovering incriminating text messages, condoms you know you did not use or don't need, being informed by a friend that they saw your husband with someone else, and so on.

Step 2: Remember how you used to react in the past.

I constantly call until I know exactly where he is. I have very long-winded conversations with him that go nowhere. Sometimes I drink until I'm no longer able to think, and then I go to bed before we have a chance to talk. Or I spew hateful vitriol towards my partner, letting him know I despise him. Another thing I keep thinking is that life is not worth it, and I should put an end to things and an end to my life.

Step 3: Think about the thoughts fueling your actions and choices.

I must somehow be responsible for his cheating. My whole life, I've noticed people are never faithful to me, and it was silly to assume it would be different with a ring on my finger. I clearly don't matter to him, but he's my whole world. He clearly doesn't feel the same, so I'm just going to give up and take my life.

Step 4: Think about new perspectives you could have about what's going on.

There's no reason I shouldn't want my partner to be faithful to me because I'm also faithful to him. It's my right to ask for monogamy and get it. There's no shame in that.

Step 5: Imagine coming face to face with the trigger and imagine that this time around, you're thinking these new, better thoughts. In your mind, play around with how you might choose a different response to help you deal with the trigger even better.

In my mind, I see myself stumbling upon evidence that he's cheating again. I feel absolutely sickened about it. I realize my thoughts might naturally want to turn to end my life as usual, but at this point in time, I will remember that I have other reasons to continue living beside this man. I have my family, my friends, and my wonderful career, which I enjoy. I look forward to a brighter future for myself. However, I acknowledge that I feel hurt right now, so I will take the time to cry and grieve. But I will not let myself feel weak or pathetic for doing so. When I'm done crying, I'll shower, feel better, get my things, and remain at a hotel or a friend's place for the night. Then I'll inform my husband that I have discovered he has been unfaithful to me once again. I will ask that he respect my desire not to be contacted, and I will seek support from friends and family. If we have to be around each other, I will do my best to give him some space so that I do not do anything that will leave me feeling regretful. I will also contact a therapist to help me deal with the trauma of being betrayed once more. To implement this plan, I need to have some cash stashed so I can stay in the hotel or at least take care of my needs as I'm in my friend's home. I'll definitely need a go bag so I don't waste time packing things up, which only gives him more than enough time to make me feel worse than I already do. It will also be helpful to have a phone with a different number that he doesn't have so that I can reach out to others without having him blow up my phone. I will contact my friends and family to inform them of my plans to seek support from them if he happens to cheat again. I will also begin looking for an appropriate therapist so that if it happens, I'm ready to begin working with them and getting better.

Now it's time for you to implement this exercise for any situation you're dealing with right now. Think about a situation or person that always triggers you and what could happen due to encountering them. Use the following format to help you.

Step 1: *Think about the trigger or triggers.*

_____

_____

_____

Step 2: *Think about how you'd react in the past.*

_____

_____

_____

Step 3: *Think about the thoughts that fuel your reactions.*

_____

_____

_____

Step 4: *Think about new perspectives you could have about the situation.*

_____

_____

_____

Step 5: *Experience the trigger in your mind, but this time, see yourself having these new and better thoughts. Also, think about how you'd have a different, better response to help you deal with the trigger effectively at no detriment to you.*

_____

_____

_____

Chapter 6

Fixing Things the Right Way

This chapter will teach you how to handle the issues in your relationships effectively. If you've always wondered if there's any way to fix the problems you face as a couple that won't leave you both with migraines and in tears, this is one chapter you shouldn't skip. If you don't take a close look at the way you get triggered or the distortions in thought that you have, you may find your attempts at problem-solving will not just fail but lead to even worse situations, making bad things worse than they already are. Fortunately, you can fix this by learning certain skills with CBT.

The CBT Fix

When it comes to CBT, these are the steps you need to follow for you to fix the issues you come face to face within your relationship:

1. First, you need to know what the problem is.

2. Next, you have to consider the options available to you.

3. After that, you must pick the best fix possible.

4. Finally, you must take action by putting the solution to work.

When trying to pinpoint the problem, you need to make sure you can't afford to be vague about it. Otherwise, the process of drumming up solutions will not be a smooth or easy one. As you think about what options you could implement to sort things out, have it in the back of your mind that no idea is too silly. Naturally, there will be times when you feel like you keep running into dead ends. In this case, it's okay for you to seek out someone else's opinions so they can help you get unstuck. However, this has to be someone mature enough not to be offended if you choose to implement other options besides what they've suggested. After this, you should consider the consequences of your choices before picking one. Finally, you need something you can do immediately to take action on your solution. It's not necessarily going to be the thing that takes care of the problem permanently, but it's what spurs you on to do all that must be done to change your situation. For instance, if your partner is not in the headspace to talk to you about something you're dealing with, you could speak with a friend while you figure out the long-term plan to deal with your partner's silence in the figure.

Note that when it's a problem that you can easily solve, your focus should be on finding solutions. But if you're dealing with something that cannot be sorted out at once because you're not the one in charge of the situation, you should forget about trying to control things or your partner and focus on controlling how you react and your feelings.

Scenario one: *Say you've always considered your partner's alcohol abuse problem yours. Then you discover through the process outlined for solving problems above that it isn't your issue. The real concern, you discover, is how your partner acts when they indulge in their habit and not necessarily the habit itself.*

First, pinpoint the issue: Your partner doesn't treat you with respect when drunk, and you notice that they tend to get inappropriate with other people, flirting with anyone around that's even a little bit attractive.

Scan for solutions: For something that will serve as a band-aid for the short term, you could let your thoughts and feelings be known to your partner now that you're aware of what concerns you. You could also look for supportive group therapy, such as Alcoholics Anonymous. When it comes to something that will sort out the issue for good, you could choose therapy to help you manage your emotions and thoughts so that you can handle your partner's drinking better, and if your pattern is open to it, perhaps they could also go to therapy. You could also learn to be more assertive with your partner so they no longer disrespect your boundaries.

Implement solutions: Think about what you can sort out right away. If you don't know how to broach the subject with your partner, you could seek support from those in your situation and ask them questions. You could look up different therapists and see which one you vibe with who knows their onions regarding codependency. After this, you could turn your attention to more permanent fixes, such as learning to communicate better with your partner in a way that doesn't exacerbate the problem and attending therapy for long enough to grasp how to deal with things.

Exercise 1

> *Kane and Leslie are newlyweds, having tied the knot just a few months ago. Kane just lost his mother, and she left behind quite a sum for him to inherit. Leslie runs a business and wants Kane to put some of his money into it so she can finally make some progress, as the bottom line hasn't been looking too great. She says she doesn't need much, but Kane drags his feet because he doesn't think it's a good idea. He has no knowledge about how Leslie runs her business, and it doesn't help that Leslie keeps bringing up the subject all the time and is now claiming that Kane clearly doesn't love her or support her, or else he'd invest in a heartbeat. She also likes to remind him that she'd never have thought twice about it if it were the other way around and he needed the money.*

First, pinpoint the issue: Clearly, Leslie would like Kane to make an investment. Kane isn't okay with doing so blindly and is also worried about letting Leslie know. Leslie is becoming more difficult to talk to, making Kane feel like he doesn't know what to do.

Scan for solutions: One of the best things Kane could do right now is to have a conversation with Leslie to let him take a look at the books, so he knows what he's getting his money into. He could ask to meet and discuss with the accounting department or ask for more time to study the industry Leslie's business is in. Kane would also benefit from getting the services of an independent financial adviser or auditor to let him know if the investment is worth it. Another thing he should do is let his wife know that it doesn't feel great when she uses his willingness to invest or not as a benchmark for whether he loves her. It's okay for him to refuse her. It doesn't have to be the end of the world. He also can invest a bit, even if he might not be sure about it. In the long run, the couple would do well from seeing a therapist to help them see eye to eye regarding money matters. Kane could also ensure his investment is made correctly, with all the procedures necessary to ensure he doesn't lose everything if the company doesn't work out.

Another thing Kane could do is make a list of the pluses and minuses regarding the various solutions he could choose. It could be that Kane realizes it's not a good idea to say no because this would lead to more drama. Besides, he loves his wife too much just to deny her. So, Kane's aware there needs to be a long, serious conversation, as that would be the better option. Having said this, he knows that when talking to a financial adviser, only good things can come from that. Yet, it worries Kane greatly about asking for the company's financials because Leslie might assume her husband thinks she can't run her business. Kane doesn't want to bruise her ego. So, he resolves to speak with her first before bringing in an adviser, and if things aren't looking too good, therapy is the next step.

Implement solutions: Kane decides that he and Leslie will speak as soon as possible about his worries. He will make it clear to her that she always has his support and that he simply feels the need to be financially responsible with the windfall they just received. Depending on how this conversation goes, Kane will know the best solution to handle the issue over the long term. He realizes that whenever he talks about what bothers him with Leslie, she doesn't handle it well. She also plays the "what's yours is mine" card, which makes Kane feel pressured. So, he checks in with his wife to see if she wouldn't mind him poking around the company's books so he can be better educated and that he intends to have a financial expert look at it with him as well. However, she isn't open to that. This makes Kane see that he has no choice but to keep his money rather than plunk it into something he knows nothing about. So, he lets Leslie know it's not okay for him to do that, and he wouldn't do that with any company without legal and financial safety nets. If Leslie still refuses to cooperate, the next and only thing Kane can do is suggest they both go to therapy to help them deal with whatever is keeping them from moving forward on the issue. Also, if Leslie still won't go to therapy, it becomes obvious Kane must work on managing his emotions, seeing as there's nothing further he can do about the situation.

Exercise 2

You've decided you'd like to take some courses because you would like to give yourself a chance to ascend the corporate ladder. You and your partner have just one car you share. To keep things convenient, you both drew up a plan. Your partner has to take you to your classes and come back for you night after night, about 5 minutes after your class is done. For some reason, your partner is an hour late. You've sent a few messages and tried to call, but it's all been in vain. You decide to look up where they might be through the tracking app installed on your phone connected to the car you share. You realize the car is parked at your partner's friend's home, where you know they're likely drinking. You are concerned because it's getting late, and you're still outside while your partner's out having a good time with a few too many drinks.

First, pinpoint the issue: Your partner has failed to fulfill their part of the agreement you made. On top of that, your calls and texts are being ignored, and as it grows darker, you can't help but worry about attracting the wrong sort of attention as you wait for them.

Scan for solutions: You must think about what you can do now. Is there a friend in the area who you could call for help? Could you try to get a ride with a ride-hailing app? What about heading somewhere safe where people are in numbers? And how about in the future? Can you both make sure you're never left stranded like this again? You should be the one to drive to class yourself and let your partner figure out when you have to go. Or you could make peace with using an app.

Implement the solutions: Focus on the moment. You shouldn't have to walk all the way to your house or where your partner is because the odds are you'll feel resentful for having to do that. If you can't afford to hail a ride on your phone, you could reach out to a friend or two and see who will be able to help you by picking you up or sending a ride your way. Next, think about what you will do to keep this from happening in the future. If you could each have your personal vehicles, you would have already, but clearly, finances are a struggle which means that isn't an option. You also may not be able to get a cab every time you want to go to your classes, so you need to look for an alternative that won't break the bank. It could be that you and your partner decide you should be the one driving the car when you've got classes.

Exercise 3

You and your partner have been together for two years and would like to move in together. To make this happen, you've both decided to set some money aside, so you create a joint account that you know is for nothing other than paying the rent and furnishing the apartment. You've also looked for creative ways to cut down on your personal expenses so that you can channel the money toward your goal. You've been saving for at least three months, and you've got up to $5,000. You're well on track to having a home together. You love to watch the money pile up, so you decide to check the account's status only to find only $500 in your account. What happened? Do you wonder if you misread the figures the last time and added an extra zero where it didn't exist?

Confounded, you check out the most recent transactions and see that your partner has been generously dipping into the money for the most frivolous things: Hotels, pricey meals, drinks, and so on. Your partner went out of town for a bit to visit their siblings, and you didn't think for a moment they would fund that trip with your account.

First, pinpoint the issue: Your partner blew most of the money on things they didn't have to, and this money was a joint contribution, which means they should have asked you before dipping into it. You'd both agreed that no one would touch the funds in it unless it was for something serious, and not without consulting the other person. However, your partner didn't keep the promise they made you, so you're set way back on your plans to have a home together.

Scan for solutions: If you want to sort out your short-term issue, you need to speak with your partner immediately. You could wait until they get back, and you can talk about it because you're dying to know if there's any of that money left. Who knows, they may have another account they temporarily couldn't access and be hoping to replace the money. Will their siblings give him some money? They're pretty wealthy and do that every now and then. You have to talk to them about what's going on with the money and the fact that they broke your trust, which means they don't care that deeply about moving in with you. You also need to do what you can to ensure neither of you can access the account until it's time to get a place.

Implement solutions: You do the first things first by waiting to speak with your partner as soon as they're back and rested. You make sure to take the time to rehearse what you'd like to tell them as you talk about the fact that the money is gone and that they broke your trust. You speak with them that night when they're back without delaying longer than necessary. For the long term, you decide you'll figure out a plan to keep the dipping from happening once more, and you both brainstorm on the matter. You both decide it would be best to cut up all cards connected to the account so that no one can make easy purchases or withdrawals.

Putting It to Work

Now you know the proper way to solve the common issues in your relationship. But knowing is only half the battle. You have to practice all you've learned. So, think about a problematic situation that isn't letting you have rest in your relationship, and then complete the exercise to come.

First, pinpoint the issue:

_____

_____

_____

Scan for solutions: What can you do in the short term? What are the options? How about the things you can do for the long term? What actions could you take to ensure you never find yourself in this pickle again?

_____

_____

_____

Implement solutions: pay attention to what you can do right away, and only after that can you focus on your long-term plan and work on how to make it happen.

_____

_____

_____

Chapter 7

Fighting and Feelings

This chapter will teach you how to deal with your feelings whenever you and your partner don't see eye to eye. Often, arguments can make you feel out of sorts and stressed out, which implies that you won't be able to let your partner know what you need from them as clearly as you can without resorting to passive aggressiveness or manipulation. You also will not do a great job hearing them as they let you know their needs. For this reason, you need to know how to handle emotions as they course through you so that you don't lose sight of each other's needs and possible ways to meet them.

If you're going to be in a relationship, you have to accept that you and your partner will have a difference of opinion every now and then. It doesn't matter if you're both mirror images of each other. You'll still have misunderstandings and conflicts, and that's okay. You'll know you're doing better with your codependency when you've mastered dealing with the uncomfortable feeling associated with inevitable conflict, letting yourself and the other person draw closer to each other. It's inevitable that by handling distressing emotions, you'll be able to understand the other person more, and they'll be encouraged to do the same for you. Many people think there's honor in never fighting in your relationship, but that's not the case. It's not like arguments won't come up or never should. When they do, you handle them as maturely and effectively as possible so that, in the end, you and your partner are more intimate with each other than ever before. Note that it's not easy to let down your walls and let your partner know what you need from them, especially when there's the chance that they will let you down. Still, you cannot deny or dismiss your needs, as they're your essence. Also, there's no way your partner can recognize and fall in love with your authentic self if you don't express what you need.

When letting the other person know your needs, you must be mindful of how you word things. Put differently, you should speak assertively, be clear about what you want, know precisely what it is, and make sure you phrase things as politely as possible so you don't hurt the other person. The trouble with being codependent is that you may not have learned to be clear in your messages, which makes you passive. Also, you may not have learned the importance of being kind while drawing boundaries, implying aggression veiled by passivity. Therefore, you need to learn to do the opposite: Be clear and kind. This way, you don't have to worry about arguments getting to critical points where everyone loses their head and says things they'll regret later. Also, being clear and kind will make fixing anything broken later on much easier.

Dealing with the Flood

Whenever it seems as though something dangerous is around the corner, it's natural to have certain mechanisms in the body and mind kick in. For instance, if your partner appears to be in a foul mood, has needs that are a tad difficult, or would like to share some criticism on how you could do better, you may feel those mechanisms kick in and get the sense of being overwhelmed. When this happens, you either want to fight, flee, freeze, or fawn. You can tell you're in this state when your heart rate goes up and you're not breathing as deeply as usual, which demonstrates that you can't communicate clearly, hear what your partner is truly saying, or empathize with them. When you get to this point, all you want to do is protect yourself. This process is known as flooding, and it happens to everyone, codependent or not.

When you're buried in the flood, you must first find a way to relax so you can move into a better frame of mind. Don't try to keep the conversation going because that would be counterproductive. Instead, you should be all about finding relief. Don't ever think that remaining in the quarrel is better than taking space to soothe yourself so you can think clearly once more. If you think about it, you can relate to the flooding experience, especially when it follows right on the heels of a difference of opinion being expressed. At this time, you should take some time and space apart. It's a good idea to speak with your partner before you get into your next disagreement about needing to have a time-out whenever the pressure worsens. It's a good way to de-escalate things.

Please, make sure you have this conversation before you get into an argument, and make it clear to your partner exactly what you'll do and say when you need some time and space. Let them know what to expect. For instance, you could have a safe word to remind you both that you're getting overheated and use it when that happens. Think about where you would like to go in your home to get some space apart from each other, and plan how long you'll take that space. Anywhere from 10 minutes to half an hour should do the trick nicely. Part of your plan should be to pick somewhere you can both come together to talk when the dust settles. The last thing either of you wants to do is stonewall the other, not if you want your relationship to last as long as possible. So, if one partner doesn't like to speak, won't listen, or takes off when you don't see eye to eye, you may need to speak with them or see a therapist to help. Time out matters because it keeps you from stonewalling your relationship to its end.

Why Breaks and Space Are Good

When you're in the middle of a disagreement, you should pull away because you have to bring yourself back to your emotional baseline. To calm down like this, there are certain coping skills you could work with, which you'll learn later in the book. When you're feeling much better, it's okay to seek out your partner once more and try to have the conversation you were having before, but in a kinder way where you seek to understand them as much as you want to be understood. At this time, please be clear about what you need, and make sure your partner knows your intention is to understand where they're coming from. To do this effectively, you must practice active listening instead of listening only to respond. When it's time for you to respond and show them you've understood them, you should communicate with the same words they used when telling you about their point of view or what they need from you. Also, you need to draw on your sense of empathy so that you can feel what they feel. Remember, the other person's point of view may be different from yours, but it's just as valid and deserves just as much attention and understanding as you'd expect to have from your partner about yours. You're about to learn exactly how to do just that. It's important to remind yourself that the way you see things will always be different from everyone else's perspective, and you shouldn't feel the need to try to change someone else's mind because that's codependent behavior. If you keep trying to prove your partner wrong, the only thing you will successfully achieve is to repel them, and this will damage whatever intimacy you have left. Your goal is to find a balance between your perspectives, which means being willing to negotiate.

Scenario 1

Assume you and your partner have had to live apart from each other because of work. So naturally, as the holidays approach, you are very happy to be able to see each other at long last since it's been months. But only will you get to see your partner for the holidays. You'll also see your family, which you've always done traditionally. In fact, your parents are very excited to meet your partner, and you let your partner know this. However, there is a problem. Your partner has their own family, who expects them to show up for the holidays, and they've already committed.

Managing Feelings and Conflicting Perspectives

Step one: Pinpoint your needs. In this situation, it is evident that you've got to spend time with your family.

Step two: Keep a cool head as you communicate with your partner. Here's what that looks like in practical terms.

- You must first ensure that you give yourself enough time to respond to the situation. This is because you likely will have noticed that you're not feeling particularly happy about this new development. You had built up an idea of how the holiday would go when it turns out your partner will not let it happen that way. However, you remind yourself that it would be unfair to impose your own desires on them and that they've also got their obligations to their families, so there's got to be a way to figure things out.

- Pay attention to your emotions as you communicate with your partner. You should tell them how you feel about the situation rather than harbor resentment by burying that emotion.

- Validate your partner's emotions. Obviously, if you're feeling frustrated about the situation, so is your partner. As you communicate with them, you must let them know that you understand precisely how frustrated they feel.

- Maintain self-awareness and self-respect. Let your partner know you're aware you both have to brainstorm a solution together because you each have to spend time with your respective families, and therefore you need to find a way to ensure everyone can continue with their holiday traditions even in the future.

- Pay attention to the other person and respect their feelings. To do this, you can reiterate that you know how important it is for them to see their own family.

Step three: Express yourself and then let go. Let your partner know you are seeking something that will work well for both of you. You must always remember that it is within your prerogative to express your feelings without being afraid of backlash from your partner. Let's assume tickets to fly over to see our partner's family have already been bought. You, in that case, should definitely inform your partner that it is important for them to let you know their plans for you before making decisions for both of you. However, in the meantime, you could make sure the tickets don't go to waste and that you find some time you can spend with your family. Remember, this step is not just about expressing yourself but also about letting go. Once you've expressed your feelings and thoughts, you need to release everything. The next thing to do is to think about how you can soothe yourself because you're clearly feeling frustration and disappointment. You may take a walk, work out, take a nap, or do something you love. You could also reach out to your family or a good friend so you can vent and let go properly.

Scenario 2

You and your partner recently talked about how much they drink and agreed that it might be a problem. Not only that, but they were also willing to put the brakes on it for just a bit. You got the sense that that was the first conversation you had had where there were no disagreements, and you might have been on the same page. However, not a week after that, your partner comes home drunk and late from work. Naturally, this makes you feel frustrated with them and rather upset. So, you let them know and asked them about their plans to stop drinking. Naturally, your partner feels attacked, so they don't react in a good way because they get the sense that you are nagging. This only upsets you further, but you try to keep calm as you gently remind them that they have committed to doing better regarding their drinking problem. Being in a completely different headspace than when you both have that conversation, your partner responds. That's what you think of as a problem is nothing since they've got it under control. Then they told you that they're simply exhausted with how controlling you are and how you continually try to manipulate them to do everything you want. They tell you that they no longer enjoy their relationship with you because you appear to be a much different person than they initially met. Naturally, this conversation leaves you feeling very hurt, but you're also aware that it would be counterproductive to engage in a serious argument with your partner at this point because it will not fix anything and would only make the matter worse. You also know from experience that the fact that your partner is drunk means that this entire conversation will be completely forgotten by them come morning. So, you decide it would be in your best interests to wait until the next day to continue this conversation when tempers are cooler.

Managing Feelings and Conflicting Perspectives

The first thing you decide to do is to take a break so that you can handle the way you are feeling. Once your emotions calm down, you go through the steps below.

Step one: Pinpoint your needs. What you need at this point is for your partner to be more sincere in their efforts to stop drinking. They need to understand that they can't just make a promise and break it whenever it's inconvenient. Also, it is your desire to feel like you are safe in your relationship, which means you should be able to let your partner know your worries and concerns without being afraid that they're going to lash out at you the way they did that night.

Step two: Keep a cool head as you communicate with your partner. Here's the practical application of this step:

- You must first ensure that you give yourself enough time to respond to the situation. You know that continuing the argument with your partner while in their drunken state would not yield anything productive. So, you decide it would be best not to spend the night in the same room. While taking time apart from your partner, you write down everything you feel in your journal to vent and calm down. Expressing your emotions in your journal means you can do so from a less defensive stance when it's time to have a conversation with your partner.

- Pay attention to your emotions as you communicate with your partner. In your journal, you note down what you think is important to communicate to your partner. You also inform your partner that you'd like to have a conversation with them the next day when they feel clear-headed. You notice that your heartbeat is fast and that you're also breathing shallowly, so you realize that you are just about to get flooded. To counter this, you begin to breathe deeply. This way, you are not overwhelmed by the storm of emotions inside you.

- Validate your partner's emotions. You realize clearly that your concerns are coming off as nagging to your partner, which could also be really upsetting for them.

- Maintain self-awareness and self-respect. What you need from your partner is more honesty and faithfulness when it comes to the promises they make you because they have a habit that causes you to feel so much fear and anxiety over the future of your relationship. So, you inform your partner that the way they act is not respectful of you or your relationship and that it's never a good thing when they drink because arguments inevitably follow. You inform your partner that you're constantly worried and hyper-vigilant about anything that could go wrong whenever they're drunk. You make sure to clarify that it is your partner's prerogative to drink if they want to. However, you are simply being clear and direct about how their habit affects you. Therefore, you would rather that they were honest with you about their habits so that you can make concrete plans to deal with your feelings whenever they drink.

- Pay attention to the other person and respect their feelings. For this part of the exercise, you gently remind yourself that your partner is an adult, and it is still right to drink. You must completely and truly accept that they are the ones in charge of their habits. You also have to realize that what you're really looking to achieve here is not to be disrespected each time they get drunk and to deal with your feelings of frustration and anxiety in a much more effective way.

Step three: Express yourself and then let go. In practical terms, here's what this looks like:

- You realize it is your right to safely express yourself without expecting any backlash. When a relationship takes two people to make it work. Therefore, it is completely fine for you to let your partner know how you feel, what you think, and what you need from them. Let them know about what you understand from their perspective.

- You know that once you've expressed yourself, you can release. Now that you and your partner have discussed how they're drinking, causing you so much pain, you can let it go. In fact, if you're going to have any peace of mind, you need to relax and let go because you cannot control someone else. However, you can relax in the awareness that you have been clear and honest about how you feel. Next time you have to deal with the situation again, you can go through this process and trust that you will be able to find a solution. In the meantime, you need to find healthy ways to cope with your emotions so that it is easier and easier for you to release and let go each time.

Putting It to Work

Think about something you're going through that causes you a lot of anguish, and then use the exercise below to help you get through it.

Step one: Pinpoint your needs. Going forward, what do you need right now and in the future?

_____

_____

_____

Step two: Keep a cool head as you communicate.

- Give yourself as much time as you need to respond. Notice your emotions as you communicate, and pay attention to your body and breath to grasp your feelings better.

- Notice and validate the other person's emotions. This means listening to them with the intention of understanding and letting them know you understand them.

- Maintain self-awareness and self-respect. This means you continue to be aware of your needs and find a way to meet them.

- Pay attention to the other person and respect their feelings. This implies you should beware of what they need from you.

_____

_____

_____

Step three: Express yourself and then let go.

- Know that it's well within your rights to express your feelings safely.

- Expressing yourself means releasing everything about the situation and the other person.

- Look for ways to soothe yourself.

_____

_____

_____

Chapter 8

Finding Peace of Mind

In this chapter, you'll discover the importance of remaining peaceful in your heart. At the end of the day, the codependent person could gain a lot from having a calm, centered mind. Mindfulness is about focusing on what's here and now and being okay with it instead of wishing it were different. Mindfulness is very important because it helps you realize that no matter how upset you get about things, that's not enough to change things. We live in a world where society glorifies the ability to multitask. The definition of productivity is the ability to do so many things at the same time. However, that's not the case at all because what winds up happening is that everything you do is subpar or worse than it could actually be. Mindfulness is important because it emphasizes channeling all your attention to one task or thing at a time.

The human mind is set up so that it naturally wanders from one thought to another without fully processing it. This is known as the monkey mind phenomenon. However, the more you practice being mindful, the better you can focus on being here and now. Mindfulness isn't about a continuous stream of consciousness grounded in the present moment and space. It is about the continuous practice of reeling your mind back in from wherever it travels to bringing it to the present moment. This is by no means an easy thing to do, and you will need to be patient with yourself as your master this skill. However, the more you practice, the better you'll get at keeping your mind here instead of worrying about the future or regretful about the past.

If you want to experience what it's like to be truly grounded in the here and now, you must immediately accept that there is no other option than to continue practicing mindfulness. Do not think of it as one quick fix you do every now and then to make things better, but as a lifelong commitment. At the beginning of your mindfulness practice, sticking to it daily is challenging. This difficulty is further exacerbated by the fact that your mind. This difficulty is further exacerbated by your mind not being used to sitting on just one topic or a center of attention. Your goal is not perfection. Your goal is simply consistency. So, the more you keep up with it, the better you'll become at being mindful. One of the beautiful things about mindfulness as a practice is that it can help you to stop being so obsessive about everything that could be wrong with everyone or yourself. Mindfulness teaches you acceptance, radical acceptance.

The Benefits of Mindfulness

Mindfulness challenges us to accept ourselves and others: If you're more mindful, you will be less judgmental and more accepting of yourself and others. This is because being mindful usually means stepping back and lessening your fixation on the things you feel guilty about. You'll become more aware that there's a critical part of your life for which you are responsible, but you are also not responsible. As a result, you'll be able to accept people as they are instead of getting so caught up with how they should live. Mindfulness also makes us more accepting of ourselves since it encourages us to see life as it really is while disregarding our preconceptions. This can help us in our relationships with others and ourselves.

Mindfulness challenges us to accept that we are not in control of everything: It is a common trait for people to think that they have total control over everything. However, we have much less control over our lives than we think. So, instead of getting caught up in the drama and fear of having no control and believing everything will always be as it is now, being mindful allows us to accept that life does not work this way. Being more aware of the challenges we face each day can help us to both accept and deal with our experiences more efficiently and effectively. Mindfulness challenges us not only to be accepting and open to change but also to be grateful for the valuable lessons that change teaches us. It requires that one be determined enough to accept things as they are. This helps to teach one self-forgiveness, which is important when dealing with life changes such as the loss of a job or lover, illness or death of those we love, and personal challenges.

Mindfulness helps you make the changes you need to be more self-actualized in life: As you start to achieve a state of mindfulness and become centered, it can be easier for you to realize that it's time for you to make some changes in your life. You'll start to feel less stressed and realize that other things must be dealt with. Sometimes we don't make those changes because we are so focused on trying to control the things that we can't change, we miss out on those we can. Mindfulness will help you notice when it's time for change and give you the courage to make it happen.

Mindfulness relaxes the body and increases awareness: When your mind is relaxed, it allows your body to relax. Much of our stress comes from having a tight grip on life, which negatively impacts our bodies. When we are mindful, we are open to our feelings and emotions and notice when we feel tense or relaxed. We can then take the actions necessary to make the changes that help us feel more at ease with ourselves and those around us. When you're more aware of how you feel at any given moment, it becomes easier for you to recognize what triggers stressful situations and how you might be able to diffuse them before they get out of hand.

Mindfulness allows you to have more control over your behavior and emotions: When you are more mindful, you will become aware of how your subconscious mind constantly tells you to react and behave in a certain way. This gives you more control over your behavior and emotions because the pressure on your mind is lessened. So, when the time comes that something triggers your inner conflict, mindfulness will give you the tools to deal with whatever it is healthily and peacefully. Mindfulness also allows you to manage your emotions by learning what positive emotions you can choose and which ones are unhealthy or destructive for you. Mindfulness helps you become more accepting of yourself and your place in this one lifetime.

Mindfulness allows you to be happier: Happiness is a choice, and mindfulness helps you make the right one. Mindfulness can help you build contentment in your life through greater self-awareness. Mindfulness helps you see things as they are instead of how you want them to be. With greater self-awareness, your life will flow more smoothly as you enjoy the good times without obsessing over the bad ones.

How to Develop Mindfulness

Practice meditation: Begin by learning a simple, calming meditation technique. Remember, mindfulness is all about being present in the moment. Meditation is a way of focusing on the present and letting it be. So, when you meditate, pay attention to your breathing or something in your surroundings without getting caught up in thoughts. Keep your thoughts focused on what you see as if it were for the first time. When your mind wanders, it will be glad you noticed and return to the object of your focus. Do this for at least 5-10 minutes at a time every day and build up over time until you can do it for longer periods. The more often you meditate, the more you can spot your codependent tendencies and check them.

Practice mindfulness when doing any activity: There are many ways to develop mindfulness. You can use any method you like both during and after the activity. As you start using this technique, make a list of things you can do at work and home, like getting up every morning and giving thanks for being alive, taking a moment to look around your workspace or room and notice the beauty of it all, and so on. The idea is to have your full attention on whatever you're doing.

Practice mindfulness as you eat: As much as possible, focus on the taste of your food instead of constantly thinking about what else you can do with your day. When eating, be mindful of your fork going into your mouth and the taste of the food. Notice the smells, textures, colors, and everything else about your food. When you've finished, notice the difference between how you felt before and after your meal.

Pay attention to how you feel in your body: This is easy enough. You can scan your body with your feet, moving up to your head. Do you notice any tension, weakness, or strength? Do you feel cold or warm? Notice the way you feel and just sit with it. Don't try to change anything.

Skills to Beat Stress

Now it's time to talk about eliminating stress or at least getting it down to a manageable level. You're going to learn some powerful skills to help you with this.

Breathing Skills: One quick and easy way to get your stress under control wherever you are is by using your breath. The great thing about the breathing technique is that you'll always have access to your breath. All you have to do is breathe the right way, and you'll be amazed at how you can deal with the stress that has plagued you through your relationship and possibly your life. When your brain perceives trouble or danger, and you get into that fight or flight or freeze or fawn mode, you stop breathing the way you're used to. You take shallow breaths as you experience flooding. Your breathing switches up on you like that because the stressful situation forces your sympathetic nervous system to kick in.

If you are a codependent person, the odds are that you have spent your entire life being stressed out, which means this is how you naturally breathe. You don't breathe as deeply as you should, which means you're always living your life on the edge, bracing for something to happen. You think your body would adapt to this form of breathing, but that's not the case. As you continue to breathe so shallowly, what's basically happening is you are causing the feelings of stress to continue even when there is no actual stressful situation to deal with. That's why you feel like you're always wired and tired. Learning how to breathe correctly with your diaphragm is a good idea.

By breathing deeply, you're waking up the parasympathetic nervous system, which means your body will stop feeling like there's danger around the corner, and you'll finally be able to relax. Breathing deeper is better. This automatically means you will have less stress, depression, and anxiety in your day-to-day life. Your brain realizes it's okay to relax, which means you can better come up with solutions to your problems in your relationships. Breathing deeply is also a tremendous help when feeling burnt out. It's a great way to revitalize and refresh your body and mind. You'll need to practice these skills to handle the distressing situations you may face daily.

Assume, for a moment, that you had the misfortune of growing up with cold, unloving parents who only ever showed you anger and disdain. This made you constantly feel on edge, ever hypervigilant, looking for the next source or cause of danger so you can quash it before it turns into an eruption of tempers that scorch you without reprieve. As an adult, you don't do well whenever you realize something you've said or done has rubbed someone the wrong way. You start to panic, and sometimes that panic gets the better of you, so you can't think of anything other than what you did. You're waiting to get some coffee when someone makes an unnecessary, rude remark. You want to speak up for yourself, but you can't engage. It feels like you're four all over again.

Step one: You can take a moment to check in with your body. Maybe you're carrying more tension than usual around your jaw and neck, and you've got a lump in your throat. You realize your fists are balled up because you want to run away or hit something. You also acknowledge that the inability to express your anger is causing hot tears to well up in your eyes.

Step two: You now recall that you're likely not breathing correctly in this present state. So, you check that and realize that's the case. You take control of your breath and slow it down, ensuring each inhale is deep, and each exhale properly empties your lungs.

Step three: You give your body another quick scan, and now you see your fists are starting to loosen up, but there's still some tension there, and you're still working your jaw. So, you breathe some more, with your attention on these areas and the intention to relax them. Now you realize that you no longer feel the urge to hit something, take off, or scream.

Step four: At this point, you can remind yourself that this person is dealing with demons and merely looking for who to project their frustrations onto. You don't have to be the one to help them feel better, not if they're going to be rude like that. They're not your problem, as it's just a random stranger in the store. You remind yourself that their rude comment is a statement of who they are, not who you are. Now, you can get your coffee without obsessing over them and its misery. You let them own their emotions without taking them on.

Positive Suppression Skill: Every now and then, people get overwhelmed. At times like these, it's perfectly okay to take a step back from the thoughts swimming through your mind and relax your firm grasp on the emotions you're drowning in. Just because a stressful situation has forced its way into your experience doesn't mean you are equipped at that moment to deal with it, nor should you be coerced into making decisions when you're not ready. Unfortunately, most people don't handle the feeling of being overwhelmed healthily. They'd rather suppress everything they feel by deliberately turning their attention to something else. Sometimes this can be a good strategy that brings much-needed relief, but indulging too often could be detrimental.

When you don't express or acknowledge your emotions, they don't just go away. Your body and mind keep score and store them. One day, one way or another, all those dammed-up emotions will come flooding out of you, either through a sudden explosion or an implosion. When it's the former, you may find yourself screaming at a friend or partner over something seemingly trivial because you've bottled up far too much for too long. If you have an implosion, the odds are you're engaging in self-destructive behavior like self-sabotage, self-harm, quitting work when you really shouldn't, getting hooked on substances, and so on. You may be tempted to think there's nothing wrong with an implosion since you're only hurting yourself, but these actions still have consequences that affect others in your life directly or indirectly.

If suppression is this bad, why even suggest it as a skill? Because when you use it the right way with full awareness of what you're doing, it can be a tremendous help. The way to practice positive suppression is to be aware that you cannot respond immediately to whatever situation you face. It's being deliberate about giving yourself some grace, space, and time to process how you feel and devise a workable solution to the problem you're facing later. In other words, you're not trying to convince yourself you don't feel how you feel, nor are you trying to ignore those emotions. You're simply choosing a time to address them and honor them when you're not too clouded in the head to do so. When you practice this form of suppression, you can naturally bring calm to your mind and body. It's like all the distressing thoughts and feelings go into a box you'll open up later to address. You have to set an exact time by which you'll address the feelings, and you shouldn't feel rushed or pressured as you sort through them. You could decide you'll bring it up with your therapist during your next session or handle the issue just before you go to bed.

Assume for a moment that you just realized your partner gave you a look that indicates they're irritated with you. Naturally, you ask them what the problem is, but they insist nothing is happening with them. This drives you nuts because there's no way for you to make progress with them if they won't talk to you about whatever is bothering them. You may then notice that you're both frustrated with how they're being non-communicative, and not only that, but you're also feeling some anxiety about what it is you may have said or done wrong this time. When you become aware of your present mental state, here's what you can do:

Step one: You breathe deeply, in and out, for three complete cycles.

Step two: You develop a thought that can help you deal with how you feel right now. For instance, you may think, "Right now, I don't feel comfortable. But that's okay. I can make peace with the discomfort."

Step three: You choose to detach from the issue completely. You realize that no matter what, there's nothing you can do to encourage your partner to speak to you before they're ready, so you'll simply wait until later in the day when they've clearly relaxed. There's no way they could sustain their foul mood all day.

Step four: When you get alone, in your mind's eye, you conjure an image of a box with a lock. As you continue with your diaphragmatic breathing, you take all the words and scenes from the distressing situation and put them into the box. You also reach into yourself, take out your frustration, anger, and anxiety, and put them into the box. You scan your body for all uneasiness, tension, or weakness. With another deep breath, you put all of that into the box along with everything else. Next, you lock the box securely and put the key in your pocket. In your mind, you pat that pocket with the intention that you will address all of this later in the day when your partner is cooler.

Step five: Practice mindful distraction. In other words, whenever you find your mind wandering off to what's happening with your partner, you simply return your attention to your work, hobby, or something that can keep you preoccupied.

Positive Thinking Skill: If you want to get ahead of distressing situations, you should teach yourself to think positively and always put a good spin on things. In other words, you must learn how to reframe things to help you. Doing this will automatically take the stress out of whatever you're dealing with. Sadly, most people have learned to be harsh critics of themselves, and their inner critic gets especially loud when they're mired in frustration and overwhelmed. This critic's voice only adds more to your stress, so it's important to learn how to silence it. The thoughts it fills your head with will vary from one condition to the next, but generally, they don't feel good. The way to shut up this inner critic is to cope with positive thoughts. Let's say you're not feeling so tough and are faced with something you don't think you could handle. You could use positive thinking as a mantra, such as, "I'm great at doing hard things." If it helps, you can even represent the positive thought that helps you as a symbol or a scene in your mind. For instance, if you're supposed to work out but can't find the will to do so, you can just say to yourself, "I'm pretty strong and disciplined. I've got this," or you could take it up a notch by seeing yourself lifting weights in your mind's eye, with the best form in the best shape of your life. You could also have pictures on your phone or around you representing the ideal you'd like to replace the negative, stressful thoughts with to help you.

Assume you've been living with your partner for almost a decade and are suddenly concerned about infidelity. This concern didn't come out of the blue, as you realize your partner is suddenly dressing better, eating healthier, going to the gym, and so on, and you get the sense that there may be someone else because they've been cold and distant towards you.

Step one: Practice mindfulness. Realize that your thoughts and emotions overwhelm you, and channel your attention to your breath or something outside you. For instance, you could try to pick out five red things in the room or notice the pattern of the sheets or the swirls on the palms of your hands.

Step two: Breathe properly. Make sure you take deep breaths that cause your stomach and lungs to fill with air as you inhale. Both should empty out totally on the exhale.

Step three: Now that your mind is clearer, it's time to craft a positive thought to help you cope with your present dilemma. For instance, it could be, "Even if the thing I fear turns out to be true, I'll still be fine. I can regulate my emotions and find peace on my own." Whenever the thoughts bother you, you simply repeat this to yourself, and you'll find yourself calming down.

Step four: Thanks to the positive thought, it hits you that you have no issues talking with your partner about your concerns. So, you speak with them, employing everything you learned from the previous chapter.

Detachment: To find peace, you should learn the art of detachment, which is about letting go of all your expectations about a person or a situation. If you have no expectations, that means you have no judgments, so it's tougher to be bothered or swayed. You take the stance that whatever will be, and you know that attempting to control the uncontrollable is futility. Detachment doesn't mean you don't have a heart or don't care about the other person anymore. It just means that you are okay with the reality of the situation. Automatically, this makes you feel less stressed out.

People tend to complain and get grumpy when they find themselves in undesirable situations, such as traffic. They worry that they will be late for something or hate that they're stuck in one spot with nothing to do other than wait. They obsess over how much better it would be if the cars would just begin moving already, but the thing is that the obsession does nothing to change the situation, and they don't realize that. However, when you're mindful of traffic, you realize that you're faced with a situation you can't control or change. If you're headed for an event, you know there's no way you won't be late, and the consequences are inevitable. You realize you feel frustrated and stressed, but you know there's nothing to do but wait. So, thanks to mindfulness, you accept the traffic as it is, which means you're not as stressed out as others in the same traffic. With this mindset, you could turn on the radio and enjoy it or enjoy a podcast or people-watching. You could also use the time to practice proper breathing.

Say you're a father, and you've lost touch with your only child. Despite all your attempts to connect with her, she won't talk to you. You're hurt because you wish you could patch things up between you two, but now, you find it's best to detach. You know you'll never stop hurting from losing touch with your daughter, but you also know it's out of your hands now.

She's the one who gets to say whether you'll have a connection, so you remind yourself, "I tried my best. Whatever will be will be." To deal with your sadness, you meditate, use your journal, work out, and you have a good cry every now and then. This allows you to suffer less and stop obsessing over how you can force or get your daughter to invite you back into her life. Detachment keeps you from losing yourself and gives you peace of mind.

Chapter 9

Getting the Help You Need

Codependency is an unhealthy psychological condition characterized by a person's extreme reliance on another person. It's not just a relationship problem but a problem within oneself. Codependent people are usually in denial and do not want to deal with their real problems. They might be full of shame and feel like they are unable to live their own life. To kick codependent behaviors, they need serious help.

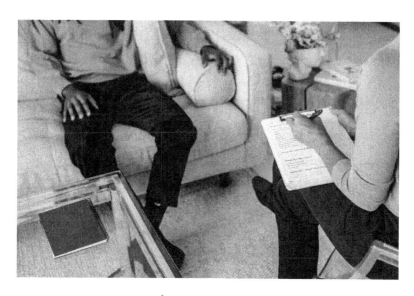

Codependency is often present in addicts' families. A child of addicted parents is usually not allowed to have their own thoughts and feelings, thus creating a population of people who are afraid of being themselves. Being different than other people scares them so much that they think everybody else is right and wrong by the same measure. They feel they must belong to something or someone to cope with their insecurity. The fear of not having someone special makes them act like objects instead of human beings.

Many codependents know that something is wrong in their relationship but cannot pinpoint the exact problem or do not want to admit it. Their problem is that they can't face the truth about themselves and their relationships. They are not sure how to stop being taken advantage of or how to begin being happy themselves instead of living only in the lives of others. They have low self-esteem, which causes them to have low self-confidence.

Many codependent people do not see a problem in their relationships, or they see something that is not great but cannot tell just how bad the problem is. For example, they might think their significant other is bad at expressing his love, but this explanation is far from the truth. The codependent could easily be dating a narcissist or psychopath, or there are so many red flags in the relationship that an otherwise healthy person wouldn't have trouble realizing how problematic that situation is.

The most important thing you can do for yourself is to decide to change your way of living. You must know that you deserve better than what you have been given or are in the process of receiving from someone else. It doesn't matter if that person is a family member or someone you met online. The bottom line is that you deserve love and empathy, not objectification and mistreatment. Once you understand this, it will be easier for you to get the help required to live a normal life again.

The first step you should take toward recovery is acceptance. You should accept your current situation and the fact that you will not be able to change it if you continue living in denial. The fear of accepting the truth about yourself and your relationships keeps you in that codependent cycle. You need to realize that your life has been affected by this condition, but you can still be happy again, just like there are codependent people who are also happy.

The next step is to get help. You need to talk to somebody. You don't have to choose a therapist right away, although it might not hurt if you did. Just talk to someone and please, try not to be ashamed about speaking about your problems. It does not matter how much that person knows about your situation. All that matters is you feel comfortable with the conversation and the person you are talking to. They might not know much or a lot, so don't be afraid of their reactions. If there is no way for you to let this out, you might as well talk to a therapist. If a therapist is what you need, look for one who specializes in codependency or addiction recovery.

Codependency is a very deep-rooted problem that can affect anyone at any age. Usually, codependent people don't know they have a problem, which makes it even harder for them to change their lives. You need to start getting help right away, and do not be ashamed of seeking the professional advice of a mental health specialist. The sooner you get the help you need, the sooner you will be able to recover from that codependent behavior and move on with your own life.

How to Stop Being a Codependent in Denial

Codependent people may be in denial even though they know their situation. The problem is that they are so used to doing things the way they have always done that they do not know how to get out of the loop. They might have tried so many times in the past and failed each time, or maybe they just haven't tried hard enough. To stop denying that there is a problem and start working on it, they need a change of perspective and a new way to go about things starting from that moment on.

The first thing you should do if you want to begin getting help for your condition is to talk about it with someone. If you are afraid of the idea, don't be. You will be much better off explaining your situation to someone who truly cares about you instead of trying to manage it alone. Remember, you deserve to recover; validating yourself will make you do it. Even if it sounds uncomfortable initially, don't let your feelings of shame override your desire for change.

The best way to stop being codependent is by taking charge of your own life again instead of depending on other people for everything. Codependency is a condition that causes the victim to think only about themselves, no matter what happens in the world around them.

As long as they continue living in that mindset, they cannot see things as they are, which every healthy person should be able to do.

A great way to start getting help is by learning to protect yourself from codependency and to separate from people who abuse you. The key lies in distancing yourself from those who cannot make you happy and cannot offer you anything of value. If you take care of yourself instead of feeling sorry for yourself, all the extra energy that would have been used in spending time on someone else will be used on growing and learning instead of being wasted on bad habits or mistakes.

What Groups Can You Join to Help with Codependency?

There are hundreds of support groups for codependent people worldwide, so you surely don't have to jump from one to another in search of guidance and help. Most of these groups are available online and off, so you have multiple choices depending on what you like and what you think will best suit your needs.

You can find any kind of group that suits your requirements, but the most common ones usually offer online or offline support by providing information about codependency, training, and education that can be useful if you want to quit the behavior. Most online groups are online discussion boards, but some are video or audio conferences that allow you to communicate with people who may or may not share your experience. You will also be able to meet others with the same problem as you and either talk about it or share their experiences.

If you want to stop being codependent and enjoy healthy relationships again, join a support group. Learn from other people exactly what your own experience has been like in such a condition so that you can avoid similar mistakes for yourself in the future. It is also beneficial if you meet others who have managed to change their lives to stop being a victim of people who are only after your money or resources. Joining such a group will help you learn from the mistakes they have made and become more aware of what exactly it is you need so that you can recover.

Preparing for Recovery from Codependency

Once you get into rehab and start learning how codependency works, it cannot hurt to read through some material on the problem. This will give you a better understanding of how this condition ties together with other things and affects every area of your life, not just people and relationships.

As you gradually start making your way out of a codependent lifestyle, it will become much easier if you have a plan to follow. Just make sure that the plan is not modeled after someone else's life and that it works for you so that you are motivated to stick with it. You can come up with this plan by analyzing the things and people in your life and deciding what role each of them plays in your life. If you end up realizing that everything related to these people hurts you, then you should choose to drop them from your life before investing any more time into relationships that are not healthy for either side.

To end codependency, you must learn to prioritize your self-care. You must stop thinking of yourself as a victim and start feeling better about yourself. That will make you feel much better about the choices that you make and the actions that you take. If you are suffering from codependency, it will be extremely difficult for anyone else in your life to see this or show them how they can help you, so it is up to you how long this condition stays with you. Of course, some people do not believe in changing their thinking and only want help for their current situation instead of trying something completely different. That is very natural, yet if you do not consider that you have to change too, codependency may be one of the things that will never go away from your life.

If you don't believe you need help with your codependence or want to learn more about it, then there are several resources that you can use. First, there is the internet with various articles and online support groups where you can get help understanding this condition and how it can affect your life in many ways. The internet is full of free information on this problem, so that is something to keep in mind if you don't have the money for any other treatment.

Of course, there are also many professionals specializing in treating this kind of dependency, so this is one more way to get information and start a program for your recovery. You will find professionals specialized in addictions, medical professionals, or even therapists with much to offer if you need further advice. There are also many books on codependency and online groups that offer support to help you if you consider yourself a codependent person but don't know what to do about it.

Why Psychotherapy Helps with Codependency

Codependency is a lifestyle that goes from one extreme to another, from complete isolation and independence to complete dependence on people and situations. That is why it is tough for codependent people to be able to find a balance in between. The good news is that there are treatments that can be beneficial when you want to escape codependency, including psychotherapy sessions which can help by teaching you how to deal with your emotions and get rid of the destructive habits you have developed so far. The help you can get from psychotherapy is important, especially if you have tried everything else to no avail and your condition seems to be worsening.

Going from being a codependent person to an independent one does not only require you to change your life, but it also requires you to change the way you think about things. That is why psychotherapy is so important in this process since it requires many perspective changes that might be difficult for you even if you want them. If instead of focusing on changing your situation, you focus on changing yourself and what goes on inside of yourself, then things will become much clearer for you.

Many people consider psychotherapy an important part of recovery because it makes them realize how much pain they have been in. Through recovery, codependents realize how much of their pain has been caused by their actions and choices. For example, if you do not take care of yourself, feed yourself healthy food, and make time for the things you like to do, you will end up feeling bad about yourself and blaming others for that. If you are depressed or anxious, you will end up blaming others for that too, and you will no longer be able to see the reason behind these feelings.

However, by adopting a more empathetic approach to your life and understanding that everyone experiences depression, anxiety, and helplessness at times, it will become easier for you to face these feelings and accept them without getting overwhelmed. This kind of self-empowerment can be seen as a form of recovery itself because it is something that most people do not have in their lives but needs to be cultivated like any other skill. Of course, the key thing to remember is that psychotherapy is not like a magic formula that will instantly allow you to break free from codependency and start living your life on a much healthier basis. It takes time, effort, and commitment to make every step toward recovery, but it can also bring you happiness and make you feel better on the other side. If you are willing to accept these changes as part of your new pattern of thinking and doing, then you should be able to break free of the patterns that have been tainting your life.

Chapter 10

Twelve Steps to Freedom

Twelve-Step programs are a common way to reach out for help whenever you have problems with substances or behaviors that are affecting your life. These programs usually offer a solution to people who feel they cannot recover independently, so they need support and guidance to become free and independent again.

Codependency is essentially the same problem because it is a condition that affects your life and leads you to make unhealthy choices. However, while being dependent on people in your life with chemicals may seem like something others can understand, being codependent also makes it difficult to see that you are responsible for your actions. This is one of the reasons why people who suffer from this condition often suffer in silence: they feel like there is no one to help them.

That is why a Twelve-Step program can be a great idea if you want to change your life and finally get out of that unhealthy relationship with your significant other, with your family or friends, or even with yourself. If you feel like you cannot do it on your own and need a helping hand, then consider this method because it can make all the difference in your life.

How to use the Twelve Steps to recover from codependency? They are not very hard to understand because they are similar to the other Twelve-Step programs. You need determination, time, and commitment to get started and ensure you know what to do.

Step One: Admitting and Accepting Powerlessness

The first step in the Twelve-Step program for codependency is ensuring that you understand that you have no power over other people. You may be codependent, but you are not in charge of them, and you cannot force them to act how you want so that you can be happy. This admission might be very humbling and eye-opening, but it is a necessary step toward taking your life back. Admitting to powerlessness means you must come to terms with the truth that the way you've been living just hasn't worked well for you. You have to finally release everything you once believed that led you to put time, energy, and resources into controlling others. When you quit the manipulation, you may find your head and life strangely empty and perhaps even boring. It could feel like you've lost a core of who you are. Also, it can be a lot to come to terms with the fact that your partner is struggling with an addiction that you truly can do nothing to fix. Note that you could be tempted to return to how you used to do things and that some people in your life may encourage you not to rock the boat. How do you deal with all that?

Step Two: Trust That a Higher Power Can Bring You Back a Whole State

Sure, you have no power of your own over others, but there's a power greater than yours which is very real and able to make the required changes. You should think about whether you've set something or someone else in the position of this Higher Power. This will likely be someone whose validation you seek, and the odds are you tend to manipulate them. The trouble is that this behavior winds up hurting you in the process. So, consider possible replacements for this Higher Power in your life. The reason it's important to have a Higher Power to turn to is that there will be times when you want to give up and go back to being your former self, and only hope and faith in this Power can pull you back from the brink. For most people, it's easy to turn to God as a Higher Power, but others think of the recovery process as the Power itself.

The thing to note about step two is that it doesn't happen all at once. It's a daily thing because not everyone is easily taken by the idea of a Higher Power. To help you with this step, consider the parts of your life that you believe need to be healed. Grab your journal and list everything you're afraid of and the steps you've taken to ensure you avoid those fears or at least have a leash on them. Then, pause and reflect on whether those methods you employed in the past were actually effective.

If you're having trouble accepting the existence of a Higher Power, you could vent about it in your journal. Feel free to ask all the questions and make all the accusations against this Power. Bare your heart and soul and hold nothing back because even as you rage against the Power, you'll find that this relieves you a lot. Also, you should begin paying attention to your life and notice the seeming coincidences that play out because those aren't ordinary events happening simultaneously. There's often more to them than meets the eye. You may also journal your journey towards believing and accepting that there's a power higher than you who you can rely on. Meditating will be useful for this step, and you should receive some direction from within you about the right steps to take going forward with your relationships. Also, consider the options you'd spring for if you had nothing to place your hopes in and nothing to be afraid of.

Step Three: Releasing

At this point, you decide that you're going to let go and trust that the Higher Power that has seen you t through life this far will take care of everything on your behalf. This means you must ask your ego to take a back seat and let the Higher Power take the wheel instead. Regardless of how you view the Higher Power or whether your ideas differ from everyone else's, you trust it to handle things on your behalf. This means you no longer attempt to control the way things turn out. You don't try to curate the way others see you in your preferred vision of yourself, and you don't give in to the frustrations you deal with that cause you to act in your old, codependent ways. It's not easy to relinquish control like this, and it's a scary affair for you, especially because of your codependence because you were unfortunately raised in a space where you experienced abuse, neglect, constant control, and other vile things. The thing to note about this step is that it's not going to happen all at once. You must take your time getting to the place of complete surrender, where you truly "Let go and let God," so to speak. Your trust is something you water, so it grows with time, and the more it grows, the easier it will become for you to move away from being codependent to being a functional, independent person.

As a codependent person, the odds are you never got to make any decisions when you were a child. Along with codependence, you struggle with doubting yourself because you never had autonomy. Since you never got the chance to make choices, you naturally aren't confident when you're forced to make one. You resort to passive ways to make things happen, including manipulation. Often, it doesn't work out well. Sometimes you do your best to keep yourself from experiencing the pain of a fear you have, and in the process, you cause that pain anyway. Or you waste precious time and mental resources thinking about everything that could go wrong (which hardly ever plays out as you thought it would). If this sounds like you, this step is really important. Turning everything over to a Higher Power will help you. If you can't trust the Higher Power completely, let it handle specific things in your life, like a test, and see how you like the results.

Step Four: Taking a Look at Yourself

You need to look at yourself for a change instead of thinking about other people. Codependency means constantly focusing your attention externally and never getting a good look at your own issues. So, this step is meant to help you fix that. When you continue to focus on others, it causes you needless pain and sorrow because you're not looking at the log in your eye and trying to get the speck out of someone else's eye. It's time to sit with yourself and realize that many of your struggles aren't because of someone else. They're your doing. The only way you can progress on your healing journey is through self-awareness. So, you should get your journal and note all the patterns you notice about yourself that do not serve you.

Please do not assume that this step is about being self-critical and harsh. It's about digging into your heart to discover the many layers of you, to see where it is you continue to stumble despite your best intentions. When you do this, you become more aware of everything about you, which means you know exactly what needs to change and how to improve.

As you look at yourself, you should know that there are good things about you and others that are not so great. So be fair to yourself. Look into every choice you've made in the past, your emotions, the things that drive you to act the way you do, and what spurs you to make the wrong choices. Don't censor yourself, but write as though no one else's going to read your entry but you. Later on, you could look at what you've got with your therapist. Note that you will need to work with someone to help you through this step. To help you, you can write down the names of those you don't like, what it is about them you don't like, and your role in the relationship. You could also write down how you feel about them, what you did in the past, what you believed drove you to act the way you did towards them, and what you can do better now. Also, write down every trait you have, both good and bad. If you can't figure it out, you can ask those in your life who should know you well enough to tell you what they think of you. Be careful not to seek out toxic people to tell you their opinions of you.

Step Five: Admitting Your Shame

The thing about secrets is that they're not always ideal. You will finally set yourself free from their destructive Power when you release them. You're meant to share every secret with your Higher Power in this step. This very intimate act requires full trust, so taking your time with this one is okay. It means you must be willing to sacrifice your ego because it will kick and scream against you revealing the truth about who you are to the Higher Power. However, it's a necessary step you must make, admitting that you're not a perfect person. You also have to make this admission not just to yourself and a Higher Power but to someone you can trust completely.

If you can't let go of the resentment in your heart and you're struggling with guilt, this step will help you. You'll let go of the shame that keeps you stuck and depressed and unlock new layers of yourself that you couldn't have found any other way. When working on this step with your therapist, you'll have to dig into your life growing up to find out what caused you pain. As you do this, you'll naturally find you're becoming someone who can walk in other people's shoes and that you're much kinder to yourself.

Please ensure that this step is done with someone you can trust. It only makes sense to choose someone you feel comfortable with who wouldn't judge you, and it's best if this person has some understanding of the Twelve-Step program so they know what's going on. Note that this isn't going to be a one-day thing, either. As you share your experiences, you may feel much relief or guilt because you realize you're not as good as you assumed you were in the past. However, you need to be compassionate towards yourself. This exercise isn't meant to shame you or make you feel terrible. It's crucial to help you become a better person, and you can do this with the next step.

Step Six: Self-Acceptance

The idea behind the program is to help you lead a less and less ego-driven life each day. So, you've accepted you have no power to control others and that there is Power, but it's not you. Next, you've decided that you're going to let that Higher Power take control of your life. You then write down every flaw you've got and everything you've kept hidden from everyone — including yourself — so you can share them with the Higher Power and a trusted person. With time, it will dawn on you that you will need a lot more than being self-aware to deal with what you're going through. You need to accept who you are if you're going to change yourself.

Change isn't an easy thing to accomplish. You may find that you continue to repeat actions that do not serve you, no matter how much you struggle and will yourself to do the right thing. Since you can no longer hide from your behavior, you find that you cannot live with yourself as you are because those actions infuriate you. Don't despair, though. There is a step to address that feeling. You just need to handle yourself with a lot of compassion. You didn't develop codependent behaviors because you're a terrible person. Those behaviors helped you survive in the past. You learned to be defensive because it was the only option to protect your self-esteem. You learned to look out for others' needs to your own detriment because it was the only way you could feel like you mattered and like you were loved. You took care of others and ignored yourself because that was how you found meaning and companionship. You let people walk all over you because you didn't know what boundaries were or that they were okay, let alone how to set them. Becoming a new person will take time, so be patient and compassionate with yourself. You can change, but it won't be because of your will. You need to accept yourself and surrender to the Higher Power who will change you.

Step Seven: Practicing Humility

Blaming yourself does nothing good for you. Thinking that you can change on your own does nothing for you. You humble yourself. It is the process of being open to the Higher Power, trusting that it can help you, and submitting yourself to its help however it comes. This step is about seeking that Power's help, and you can only do so from a place of humility, which, contrary to popular opinion, is not weakness. You've noted that you have shortcomings you may have tried to overcome on your own in the past but failed. You now know you failed because you were never the one in charge. The Power in this step is the hope it brings, the knowledge that you can become who you want to be with the help of an unstoppable force. So, all you have to do is wait and trust this Higher Power. You should find that humbling yourself is made easier because you've chosen to set aside your pride and stop hiding from being flawed. You know now that you're not in control of anyone, and from this humble position, you can accept others and yourself.

Step Eight: Pinpointing the Ones You've Hurt

You need to list everyone you've hurt and open your heart and mind to patching things up. At this point, you should be able to understand the gravity of your actions on them. You can go through the list you made with your therapist or sponsor and talk about what happened and why you've got to make it right with them. Note that this isn't the time to justify your choices. Emphasize that you hadn't meant to cause harm or anything else. It's possible to still feel some resentment towards these people, so if that's the case, you should write that down. You may feel ready to speak with some people on that list, but in the beginning, you may not find it easy to apologize to the ones in your life who hurt you terribly. In this case, you must surrender once more to your Higher Power, asking it to help you forgive them and trusting that it will. As you make your list, don't forget one very important person who needs to be on it: You. You've got to patch things up with yourself because you've spent your life blaming yourself, sacrificing yourself when you need to be addressed, and denying any problem. If you'd never want to do that to the people you love, why don't you think you deserve an apology from yourself, too? Think about it.

Step Nine: Making Things Right

This step asks that you make it right with everyone on your list when you can. You're only excused from doing this with people who would only cause you or others more pain. It's natural to feel very scared of this step, but it is necessary as it teaches you to be humble. Making amends will improve your capacity for empathy and compassion by leaps and bounds. Also, there's a sense of starting on a new page, which can be very exhilarating for you. Some of the most amazing things happen when you set your ego aside to make things work. You need to do this in person as often as possible, and when apologizing, be very clear about what you're apologizing for. Otherwise, it doesn't feel sincere.

What do you do when the person you want to make amends with has passed away? You could go to their grave, write them a letter, or talk with them as though they were in the room. You could give to causes you know they believed in when they were alive. Part of that process would involve restitution if you stole or ruined someone else's things. You should list how you intend to fix things practically with each person. Sometimes, your apologies and actions may not fix the relationship, but that's okay. It's not in your control, so surrender to your Higher Power. Also, take concrete steps to fix things with yourself. Please, when dealing with others, let go of the idea that they should react in a certain way or want anything to do with you. Sometimes they may not remember what you've done and may choose to avoid you because of their pain and anger. In the latter case, you could try a couple more times to make it right and then let it go. Note that when it comes to dealing with the abusive people in your life, they'll see your actions as a wonderful opportunity to tell you all the other ways you're a terrible person, so get ready to deal with that. You're going to fix things, not get your heart crushed, so protect it. This princess will take a while, so take your time.

Step Ten: Starting Afresh Each Day

You never stop growing and discovering yourself. The same thing applies to recovery: It's a never-ending process. You need to keep at it. So, continue to take stock of your actions, and when you have to, make amends. This is how you keep your life fresh each day. When something bad happens, don't just shove it aside because your subconscious mind will never forget, and it will come back out ugly if you keep suppressing things. Make a point to address pain points with people in your life and to apologize as soon as possible. Rather than allow yourself to feel guilty, use that emotion to spur you to take accountability for your actions and fix things. This way, you grow more in peace, empathy, and compassion. Review your life and actions each day before you turn in for the night. This way, you'll be able to keep your codependency in check until you no longer indulge in those destructive patterns. Remember not just to write about what you did wrong but what you did right, too, no matter how "small" you may think your choice was. To help you, ask yourself the following questions:

1. Was there a point when I felt resentment?

2. Did I feel fear today?

3. Was there any way I was dishonest?

4. Is there something I should share or discuss with the other person?

5. Is there someone I owe an apology to or need to make things right with?

6. What are three things I can commend myself for doing today?

7. What are the things I'm most grateful for?

Step Eleven: Maintaining Your Connection with Your Higher Power

This step requires prayer and meditation to remain in constant contact with your Higher Power, so they can continue helping you in life. When you remain in touch, you continue to seek its guidance, and in this way, you can make better choices each day. You also don't lose the self-awareness that you've managed to build over the previous steps. Connecting to your Higher Power daily is a good way to keep your ego in check and stop yourself from feeling needless anxiety and resentment. Check in with this Power first thing in the morning and last thing at night.

As you deal with your Higher Power, you should ask it to let its will be done rather than tell it what you want. This way, you don't have to struggle with disappointment. Prayer is asking for God's will to be done, which will bring you the best outcome possible, and meditation is the part of a prayer that helps you listen for guidance. The answers may not be all at once or on the first few tries, but remember to surrender and trust that they will come.

As a codependent person, you're not the most patient sort because you've learned throughout your life that you must always be doing something. This means you tend to charge into things headlong with no proper planning, and you wind up dealing with even more issues. This step is meant to teach you to stop worrying about how things turn out and stop trying to force them to go your way. It is the ultimate surrender. Note that when you get answers from your Higher Power, they will feel like the choice with the most peace and the least anxiety.

Step Twelve: Putting the Principles to Work

You have to take everything you've learned from steps one through to eleven and use them in every aspect of your life, whether that's your career, love life, health, spiritual life, and so on. You can't be honest when it comes to your relationships but dishonest with your health or in your business affairs. You can't resent one person and not resent someone else. There must be congruence in your thoughts, words, and actions.

Also, consider helping other codependents that you can help who might want to work with this program. You don't have to fix their issues, and you don't need to let them cause you sleepless nights because you're trying to stop that behavior. You should support them with their problem-solving, but don't do anything more. Don't offer advice or tell them what you think they should do. Simply be present, compassionate, and aware of your boundaries and theirs.

Conclusion

Codependency is often driven by the desire to keep other people happy, which means cutting down one's desires and feelings to suit their needs. Codependents are typically caught up in fixing the problems of their significant others because they fear that doing anything else might lead to abandonment or conflict. But this behavior ultimately leads codependents into a world of hurt in which they sacrifice their happiness and well-being for someone who will never change or reciprocate these behaviors.

If you put in the work, you'd be surprised at how radically different your life will become as you break free from codependency. It is possible if you are willing to follow through and refuse to give up. You see, codependency is a learned behavior and can be unlearned.

Codependency is the core of many people's problem-solving mechanisms, even though it causes more pain than joy. Naturally, things get more complicated when codependency is not created by choice but is instead an inherited trait that we must learn to recover from. But, if you can pinpoint the cause of your codependency, you will have a much easier time recovering from it and learning to overcome it for good this time.

Understanding codependency will allow you to decide how you want your life to be and what behaviors are required for your happiness rather than someone else's happiness. In the end, this means you will finally have a fulfilling life when you put in the work. You'll have a life where you can simply relax and trust that your existence is more than enough proof that you're worthy of happiness, joy, and all the good things in life.

Thank you for buying and reading/listening to our book. If you found this book useful/helpful please take a few minutes and leave a review on Amazon.com or Audible.com (if you bought the audio version).

References

Anderson, S. C. (1994). A critical analysis of the concept of codependency. Social work.

Cermak, T. L. (1986). Diagnostic criteria for codependency. Journal of psychoactive drugs.

Cowan, G., Bommersbach, M., & Curtis, S. R. (1995). Codependency, loss of self, and power. Psychology of Women Quarterly.

Fuller, J. A., & Warner, R. M. (2000). Family stressors as predictors of codependency. Genetic Social and General Psychology Monographs.

Irwin, H. J. (1995). Codependence, narcissism, and childhood trauma. Journal of clinical psychology.

Knudson, T. M., & Terrell, H. K. (2012). Codependency, perceived interparental conflict, and substance abuse in the family of origin. The American Journal of Family Therapy.

Lancer, D. (2014). Conquering shame and codependency: 8 steps to freeing the true you. Hazelden Publishing.

Lancer, D. (2015). Codependency for dummies. John Wiley & Sons.

Morgan Jr, J. P. (1991). What is codependency?. Journal of clinical psychology.

Mulry, J. T. (1987). Codependency: a family addiction. American family physician.

O'Brien, P. E., & Gaborit, M. (1992). Codependency: A disorder separate from chemical dependency. Journal of Clinical Psychology.

Vlaicu, C. (2020). CO-DEPENDENCY IN INTIMATE RELATIONSHIP-A LEARNED BEHAVIOUR. International Journal of Theology, Philosophy and Science

Printed by BoD™in Norderstedt, Germany